CEYLON

THE PARADISE OF ADAM

THE RECORD OF SEVEN YEARS' RESIDENCE
IN THE ISLAND

Photo 11 Ranelagh Mansions, S.W.

THE AUTHORESS

CEYLON

THE PARADISE OF ADAM

THE RECORD OF SEVEN YEARS' RESIDENCE IN THE ISLAND

CAROLINE CORNER

WITH SIXTEEN FULL-PAGE ILLUSTRATIONS

ISBN : 978-93-5324-513-9 (HB)

First Published, London, 1908

Published, 2020

Published by

Facsimile Publisher
12 Pragati Market
Ashok Vihar, Ph-2
Delhi-110052
E-mail: books@facsimilepublisher.com

Printed at: G. Print Process, Delhi.

CEYLON, The Paradise of Adam

Author: Caroline Corner

CEYLON

THE PARADISE OF ADAM

THE RECORD OF SEVEN YEARS' RESIDENCE IN THE ISLAND

BY CAROLINE CORNER

WITH SIXTEEN FULL-PAGE ILLUSTRATIONS

LONDON : JOHN LANE, THE BODLEY HEAD
NEW YORK : JOHN LANE COMPANY : MCMVIII

CONTENTS

Contents

Contents

Contents

Contents

Contents

CHAPTER XXIX

CHAPTER XXX

CHAPTER XXXI

CHAPTER XXXII

CHAPTER XXXIII

ILLUSTRATIONS

Illustrations

The frontispiece is from a photograph by the Reflectum Studio, Hurlingham, S.W., and the other illustrations are reproduced by permission of Mr. Plâté, Ceylon

C E Y L O N

THE PARADISE OF ADAM

CEYLON

THE PARADISE OF ADAM

CHAPTER I

Cynthia's arrival at Colombo—Her new home—What the Bird of Paradise told her—The Paradise of Adam: What of Eve?

CYNTHIA had only arrived in Ceylon that morning. Passing her stupendous load of luggage through the Customs at Colombo, and seeing it stowed away in a big bullock-cart for a six miles' journey, had occupied the time till tiffin at the Grand Oriental Hotel, familiarly called the G.O.H. Later on, some couple of hours, she found herself seated on the verandah of her new home, an idyllic home so far as appearances go.

"A Grecian temple set up in the Garden of Eden," she had likened it to on first beholding.

"Can ordinary mortals live ordinary lives in such abodes, amid such surroundings?" she had asked. Personally, she thought it impossible; so might any newcomer.

Now she sat—or rather reclined on a "lounger" on the broad stone verandah, covered over here and there with a few soft Indian rugs—wondering! What was her life here to be?

The heat-laden atmosphere was not conducive to speculation, however. Heavy with the scent of tropical blossoms in profusion—the orange, the myrtle, the passion flower, *rat mal* and areca, the air seemed to be possessed of narcotic properties, or was it merely fatigue that overcame and caused her to feel drowsy? *So* drowsy that when a Bird of Paradise came and peered inquisitively at her, she fancied she was indeed in the Garden of Eden, so lovely a creature surely suited this fair illusion. Cynthia's eyelids drooped and flickered as the sunbeams glinted on the proud bird's gossamer tail, flickered and drooped until they closed.

Silence. Not a sound; not a rustle. Only heat and golden sunshine and silence. All nature was asleep—slumbering in a golden bath. Even the talkative tit-willow was silent, taking a *siesta* with the crows—that noisy crew—and the sparrows—those overgrown fellows—and the little dark-eyed squirrels and tiny tortoises—all were silent, at rest.

Only this Bird of Paradise was awake and abroad. Very much awake, he trod the verandah with the air of a king, glancing every second in the direction of the young Englishwoman, whose

Photo. Plate, Ceylon

LANDING STAGE, COLOMBO, AND CUSTOM HOUSE WHERE CYNTHIA'S BELONGINGS ON ARRIVAL WERE 'PASSED'

head lay back on the soft silk cushion, whose eyes were closed in sleep.

"A newcomer, eh?"—Was Cynthia dreaming? A voice seemed to speak in silvery tones, while the little red feet of this princely bird paused in its patrol, and the beautiful shimmering tail was spread out in full view of Cynthia, had her eyes but been open to see. "A newcomer, eh? Enraptured with our lovely isle, I'll warrant, already. A contrast, certainly, to your foggy London and its dirty sparrows. Bah!"

Yes. It was the Bird of Paradise speaking, and proud as he was handsome he looked.

"Well, it's kind of you to invite us to afternoon tea. My wife will be here presently. All feminine creatures love the gossip-hour. *We* are mere escort—*noblesse oblige*. By the way, I hear that expression is becoming obsolete amongst your people. Ah! you didn't know we could talk and are given to discussing your affairs? There's something yet to learn. Perhaps even we of the jungle could teach you something if you gave us the opportunity. We often 'talk you over,' as you say, and sometimes terminate the discussion with a vote of censure on some of your ways. Whew! here comes my wife."

A dowdy little bird some might call "homely' fluttered down to the side of her magnificent mate. She had a penetrating, round, black eye, though.

That she fixed upon him. A little of the "starch" went out of him *then*, and he appeared to shrink.

"Too personal, am I? Well, that *is* bad form, I know. But, Betsy, my love, now doesn't your own blood boil when you see wholesale slaughter of our loveliest—golden orioles, dainty kingfishers, jays of the heaven's blue, parrots and parakeets—for what? To adorn the womenfolks' headgear. I saw a specimen at the King's House the other day. A—ye? Very well, Betsy, my dear, I'll say no more. Qur-rh! how the mosquitoes bite! It's not all bliss even in Paradise. You'll find that out if you stay long enough. It's the custom of the country."

"Adam, the father of all, found something wanting when driven out from Eden. He parted from Eve on the Plains of Mesopotamia prior to his banishment to Ceylon, the Paradise of Adam. Chuck-chuck!" The Bird of Paradise chuckled, but pulled himself up quickly in face of that penetrating, round, black orb of his mate.

"Yes, yes, I've got *my* wife. I'm aware of *that*, Betsy, my dear. Eve only was banished to Hadjáz, since called the Paradise of Eve. Poor Eve—no Adam! Poor Adam—no Eve. What Paradise!"

"But we are becoming sentimental; and sentiment"—turning to the sleeping girl, fresh from the world's metropolis—"sentiment's out of date.

You don't think so. The moon's made of honey still to you; the world's still Eden. All right, Betsy. I'd only have her know that *this* is the Paradise of Adam, and I, *I* am the *king*." And, turning, this beautiful creature shook out that magnificent tail so that it presented all the appearance of regal robes set with priceless gems. Then there was a flutter, the patter of bare feet, and a voice. Cynthia awoke.

"Dinner-gong, lady."

It was a chocolate-coloured man in white, wearing a "poll-comb," resting on the crown of his head, who spoke—an *appoo*, or head servant.

Cynthia arose. No bird of paradise was there, no "Betsy"—only a few remaining crumbs on the stone verandah.

The sun had set, the moon was rising. From a vision of gold the scene was changing to a dream of silvern beauty.

The birds had flown, but the verandah was aglow with fire-flies; and though many blossoms had closed, others had opened at the call of night.

"Paradise—the Paradise of Adam!" mused Cynthia. "What of Eve?"

CHAPTER II

Description of Cynthia's bungalow in the Cinnamon Gardens—A Ceylon *entourage*—Pomp and circumstance *versus* crudity—" It's never To-day, always To-morrow "—The " custom of the country."

A DESCRIPTION of this new home of Cynthia's is of paramount importance; first, in that it bears so close an association with the forthcoming narrative, secondly, because of its future use and value to other *ingenués* fresh from "home." Exteriorly then the bungalow resembled, as Cynthia said, "a temple" built on classical Greek lines. White, virgin white, all of it. Some are yellow, others pink, and so on, but these are invariably in the occupation of " natives." The European draws the line at white. White the stately pillars of the square portico, white the pillars on either side, two of them, some twenty feet, within. These four pillars lined the long stone verandah screened by closely wooded *tats* and curtained by trellised and clambering creepers, as well as carpeted by Indian matting and a few loose rugs. It was a bungalow. Consequently it had no upper storey, those that have are designated " houses " in this Paradise of Adam. In the centre of the verandah, and facing the imposing portico, was a pair of jakwood doors lofty and large, by day always wide open, except when the monsoon rages wild and furious. At top of these doors were elaborate perforations by way of ventilation and decoration both. The Sinhalese are mightily proud of these designs and achievements, and always when bargaining for the bungalow draw European attention thereto. The locks of these doors, however, leave much to be desired. Why they have locks at all is a mystery, starting from the point of their usefulness. A push and a shove and the lordliest of doors gives way, and one finds oneself in the drawing-room. Herein lie the pomp and circumstance of the dwelling—a queer combination of East and West—the bungalow being the only point where the centripetal and centrifugal forces of East and West do meet and mingle. The effect, although bizarre, is picturesque and somewhat artistic withal. Civilisation and barbarism, crudity and culture, the latter depending on the European occupant *individually*, for *collectively* culture is conspicuous by its absence in Ceylon—ancient and modern, everything antithetical and anachronal arranged together in a delightful *olla podriga* of the Orient and the Occident. All of the best is here however—the pomp and circumstance of the bungalow, and of the occupant, who, if a "Service Man" lets that fact speedily be known. As on the verandah wicker chairs and bamboo tables preponderate, those from Singapore with cushions after Liberty being very comfortable indeed. A teapoy or two is *de rigueur*, as likewise are the card table, cabinets in beautifully carved Bombay wood, whatnots, and *bric-a-brac* of the gentlewoman of to-day, that is if she determines to live as though she were still resident in, say, South Kensington, as did Cynthia—alas!

The walls are a feature of the Orient. In Cynthia's home they were "distempered" olive green, with stencillings of salmon pink, very effective and restful to the eyes. From a distance, however, the walls bore a distinct resemblance to a map in a London railway guide. Lines and lines traversed them, meeting sometimes and forming mounds that might be junctions, then diverging and continuing from floor to ceiling, from ceiling to floor, ay, and across the floor, lines of *mud*, constructed by white ants all over the *rattan* matting. A Colombo dwelling boasts of seven different *genus* of ants, each with an individual taste in the way of appetite, although *all* are *gourmands*, thence nothing falls foul of the ants, from the interior of the piano to the interior of the sugar basin, with everything between, the dining-table having to stand in wells of water on their account, and even then the white cloth is traversed by opposing regiments of them soon as laid. The ceiling—a mere sheet of *chunamed* (whitewashed) canvas stretched tightly beneath the tiles—permits of a few inches space against either wall as an exit for huge furry spiders which, when the lamps are lit, take their walks abroad from their nests in the tiles, foraging for gnats, mosquitoes and whatnot for their next day's dinner.

There is always a smell of damp and mildew in a Colombo bungalow, even though it may be in the aristocratic Cinnamon Gardens, as Cynthia's was, indeed at "Hyde Park Corner," so called! albeit, the rooms are well open to air if not always to light, for the *jalousies* must be closed to shut out the heat once the sun is in the meridian.

Again, Oriental architects are uncertain in their disposition of windows. One room may have many; another none. However, Cynthia's drawing-room had three, while a small apartment on either side, which were called respectively a "boudoir" and a "study," were all window from ceiling to floor, although the "spare room"—a large one—was windowless. "One never knows" might be an *addendum* to the tea-planter's motto for Ceylon: "It's *never* to-day; *always* to-morrow." Behind the drawing- is the dining-room—part of the pomp and circumstance, being only divided by a screen—a remarkably handsome screen of beautifully carved jakwood, reaching almost to the ceiling. The dining-room, however, boasts of an Austrian pinewood ceiling, which, though it may prevent insects flavouring your soup, certainly renders the atmosphere hotter, spite of the *punkah*. The only item distinctive, saving the *punkah*, which is addicted to St. Vitus's dance owing to the *wallah* continuously being caught napping, was the extraordinary number of soda-water glasses on the dinner-waggon and the display of delicious tropical fruit.

On either side of these pomp and circumstance apartments are the bed, dressing, and bathrooms. Cynthia's overlooked the plantain fringed lake—a truly lovely view; the others, the compound, in which trees—suryas, peepuls, papois, castor-oil, pomegranates, sugar-cane, cocoa-nut, date and areca palms flourished; while bougainvillæa, beaumontias, pine-apples, pumpkins, cucumbers (large as vegetable marrows), with trailing columbine and begonia formed a luxuriant tangle over a carpet of orchids and blossoms that spring up in a day and make a cool and cosy couch for snakes. Right in front of Cynthia's bungalow was what to her was its glory—to the gharry-passengers a marvel—to wit, a flambeau tree. Twice a year its far-reaching branches were pendant with blossom. Such blossom! Bell-shaped, each fell from each branch several feet in length, in colour red, brilliant as fire. Over the roof, over the entire front compound, the branches stretched, a gargantuan umbrella of fiery blossoms—a veritable sight to behold. This was Cynthia's new home.

And now a word for the household economy. Practically it was in the hands of the *Appoo*, or head servant, called by Europeans unaccustomed to such a functionary (often as not, may be, to any household help whatsoever), "my butler." The *Appoo* is, indeed, not merely a star of the first magnitude, he is a sun, around whom all the domestic system revolves. Cynthia was inclined to be a bit afraid of such a mighty personality. He had been her husband's servant for seven years. Brides, beware of these bachelor factotums! House-boy, dressing-boy, coolie, even the *ayah* is subservient to him. Not so the cook, who is a law unto himself and a terror over his "mate" or assistant; not so the *Muttu*, or horsekeeper, who only makes his appearance twice a day at the back verandah door in order to exhibit the "paddy and gram" prior to giving to the horse, as he would say—previous to purloining, as Cynthia soon found out. The duties of the "cook's mate" comprised washing plates and dishes, cups, saucers, &c., &c., in a wooden bucket on the back verandah in water rich as the best mulligatawny, the secret of which lay in the fact of its never being changed; and of playing "understudy" to the grandiloquent *Madrasee* at those times when the culinary regions reeked with *arrack*. *Dhobie* and garden coolie resided not on the premises. The *Muttu* and wife or wives did—in the stable adjoining the horse, mats taking the place of straw.

So much for the domestic economy, which, however, is very subject to change when a European lady takes the reins in hand, as Cynthia's soon did. Bachelor bungalows are run on different lines.

"It's like the old game of family coach with these native servants," remarked Cynthia, after about a month's experience, "always one or other on the move."

"It's the custom of the country" was the reply.

CHAPTER III

Forbidden fruit: and consequences!—Sherry for the pudding—How Cynthia first violated those "customs of the country"—A weird awakening—"Bad devils" and their "ways" in his Majesty's First Crown Colony, otherwise The Paradise of Adam.

WEEKS passed by. Cynthia was instated in her new home.

"It's not the custom of the country."

This, to Cynthia, appeared to be the text on which all one's actions in this new strange land should turn. Now her broad mind rebelled at restrictions—"cramping," she called them. For instance, the regions of her home beyond the back verandah being sacred to the native servants, no European foot should enter there, she was told. On Cynthia's skull there was a bump, not of inquisitiveness, but of love of adventure. Accordingly, when the servants had taken themselves off, which they ought not to have done, Cynthia determined to indulge this characteristic, "customs of the country" notwithstanding. And she did. *That evening Cynthia ate no dinner!*

The cook, a Madrasee and a fine figure of a man, was, withal, excellent in his own way. Soup, fish, *entrées*, sweets, with curries galore—all were unimpeachable, as were his immaculate white suit and Turkey-red turban. This description applies to *Keribunda* on view; *Keribunda* in private was an altogether different personality. Once Cynthia set eyes on him in private—and flew. His appearance defies description, as does that of a Ceylonese kitchen, wherein toothsome luxuries and daintiest of dishes have birth—along with myriads of insects and multi-myriads of odours, each more noxious than the other, all arising from putrefying refuse heaps. It was not this, however, that made Cynthia fly; it was the soup, that excellent wine-like soup being strained through *Keribunda's* loincloth!

Alas! for having partaken of the forbidden fruit of knowledge!

Keribunda's sweet puddings were delicious. Perhaps they ought to have been; *Keribunda* was always sending the *podyan* (boy) for a "little sherry for the pudding, please, lady;" so often that a bright idea occurred to Cynthia's as yet unsophisticated mind. "Here is one glass of sherry *for the pudding*, and another for cook—tell him." An inspiration, however, that did not answer. The request came oftener, and with it a distinct falling off in the quality of the pudding.

Cynthia had much to learn *re* the customs as well as the *non* customs of the country.

Now, Cynthia was naturally a light sleeper. Her slumbers soon came to be disturbed between 1 and 2 a.m., when she heard voices in the compound. On mentioning it, the answer she got was, "Natives walking to Colombo. They prefer to walk at night; it's cooler. Try not to notice it. You'll soon get accustomed to it."

"How clear the atmosphere must be for sound to be so audible at such a distance," she was thinking, for the compound was a large one.

Next night, or rather morning, she awoke and listened. Surely those voices were nearer than the road. She was half inclined to get up and reconnoitre. But black faces and forms in the black darkness of silent night are not such commonplace things as they are by day.

When she spoke of it next day, her husband, looking amazed at her half-formed resolution to get up and reconnoitre, said, "On no account. Wake me next time."

This she did—next night.

"S—sh!" once he was well awake. "Our cook's voice, by George! What's he up to? Where's my gun?"

"Don't—pray don't; it's not so serious as that," pleaded Cynthia in a whisper. Women have such a horror of firearms. "Let us put out the lamp and peer through the *jalousies.*"

The stone verandah stood out in the darkness of night; so likewise did the white raiment of some dozen natives asquat, each with a plate of curry and rice, into which some two dozen black hands dipped, while the lordly figure of *Keribunda* towered majestically above them all.

"A restaurant for vagabonds, eh! I'll settle the rascals." The gun was requisitioned now.

"Don't *load* it!"

But Cynthia's entreaty was drowned in the wrenching open of the back verandah door.

"Cook? *Keribunda?* Hi! ho! there." Not a sign nor the vestige of a human being was there. Bang! bang! bang! It was only the butt end of the gun on the kitchen door. No response. The one little opening which did duty as a window revealed nought but darkness within. All was silent as the grave.

Bang! bang! bang! again. Again no response.

"Unlock the door or I break it open."

"I thought I heard a snore," whispered Cynthia.

"Yes. Don't you hear? He's sound asleep."

"Open the door or—I'll fire through the window."

Now a movement suggestive of a stretch—followed by a blunderborean yawn.

"He's awake. Don't fire, pray," said Cynthia.

Then the key turned in the lock, and the figure of *Keribunda* with drapings *degagés* presented itself. Too sleepy presumably to take in the situation, *Keribunda* gazed, then yawned, then rubbed his eyes and gazed again, then yawned—bewildered.

"Where are they? the rest of the rascals? Speak, or I'll——"

"Master speaking I not understanding. No rascal here. Gentleman's house this," at last *Keribunda* woke up sufficiently to say.

"Yes, and you make of it a restaurant for vagabonds. Where are they, I say?"

"I not knowing rascals, vagabonds, sar. I gentleman's servant—high-class Madras cook."

"Where *are* they?"

"Master saying p'raps I drunk, I not understanding. Lady know, sar, I telling no lie. Good Christian man I bringing always from bazaar."

"Tush! Where in God's name have the rascals got to? Tell, and I—I'll look over it this time."

"I telling master if master come look. Not in kitchen, master see. Not there. Master come 'way, I telling master. Lady hear, lady get 'fraid."

"Don't go—*far*," from Cynthia, shaking.

"All right. I have the gun. The sight of it's enough. You go in."

As the two moved aside :

"Sar," said the Madrasee mysteriously, "big devil come, walking round the bungalow. Every night that devil come, sar. I want tell master, but lady know lady get 'fraid. Very big, bad devil that, sar."

"But there was more than *one* voice?"

"Master not knowing ways of bad devils. Bad devil many tongues got. All many tongues talk together. Many tongues this bad devil got, sar, ve—ry many."

"I should like to see him. Where is he?"

Keribunda shook his head gravely.

"Gone, that bad devil, no more wisible."

"H'm! Then next time he comes I'll greet him with powder and shot."

But, alas! that greeting had not a chance of coming off. Next day *Keribunda* having received his "pay" and a little "advance for clothes" befitting a "gentleman's house" became likewise "invisible," as also did sundry little things that became the property of *boutique* keepers, who invariably indulge in double dealing literal as well as figurative. Both "customs of the country" the European soon becomes acquainted with, if not quite reconciled to, in His Majesty's First Crown Colony—otherwise the Paradise of Adam.

Photo. Platé Ceylon

A STREET IN THE CINNAMON GARDENS, COLOMBO, WHERE CYNTHIA LIVED WITH RICKSHAW AND WALLAH AWAITING

CHAPTER IV

Cynthia's early morning mount—King's House and Mrs. Grundy—First ride in a bull-hackery—Moonlight of Ceylon — A genuine *Yakkadura* (Devil-Dance)—*Diablerie* and its fascinations—A *Taincama* under hypnotism restored to her normal condition —The weirdness of weird ceremonies : from midnight till "magpie" morn.

MOST of all Cynthia delighted in her early mount. Before the sun had risen she was in the saddle. This is the time to see and to enjoy that most beautiful island Ceylon. Far out among the little native villages she would ride, unaccompanied except for the company of her faithful little dog. The Europeans she encountered later on her return stared and may be wondered, "Where had she been? What business could a European have, a gentlewoman too, beyond the prescribed limitations of the Park or Galle Face Drive?" Little did they dream of the interest these solitary expeditions had for that eccentric English girl, as doubtless she was called. Those primitive villages are teeming with interest, did the European but know or care. Old world superstitions, queer rites and quaint ceremonies are still believed in, still observed, while the many evidences of true artistic taste must or should appeal to the cultured and the æsthetic. As gems are discovered buried amongst mud, so jewels of spiritual worth may be found amid the filth and ignorance of so-called "heathen" Oriental village life. The Asiatic—particularly the Sinhalese—is reticent, because he is suspicious of the European, deeming his interest—when he has any—curiosity idle, if not dangerous.

One morning, however, Cynthia chanced to fall in with a native *Mudaliyar*, a learned man as well as a sort of local mayor and magistrate—the translator also of some of the sacred books of the East. This man to Cynthia proved a mine of wealth. Was the lady indeed interested? Personally this native *Mudaliyar* confessed he had little interest in the "fantastic ceremonies," still held and believed in by the "simple villagers." His daughter was a Christian, he went on somewhat proudly to tell. Of course Cynthia was glad to hear that, all the same she was very keen on drawing the learned *Mudaliyar* out. This she did, with the result of a promise being given to assist this English lady in her studies of Oriental rites, beliefs and occult practices. This promise was fulfilled.

Cynthia had of course heard of devil dances,

but none of the stories she had read concerning them explained their *raison d'être*, or esoteric meaning if there were any. Here was a chance of seeing for herself and learning the truth, a chance not to be missed. The miscellaneous ladies attending King's House might shudder with horror, Cynthia resolved on attending a *Yakkadura*—a genuine devil dance, not one got up on the verandah of a European's bungalow as a novel entertainment and excitement for the distinguished visitor or the globe-trotter.

On a certain *poya*, that is full moon night, Cynthia, accompanied by her husband, took her seat in a bull-hackery in accordance with the fitness of things, and irrespective of the "customs of the country," dictates of Mrs. Grundy, and all else besides save her Cynthia's own delight in having this chance of beholding one of the strangest and most interesting sights in the world.

Previously a Sinhalese astrologer had informed her that the times most favourable for occult rites are new moon, half moon and full moon, designated *poya*. At these seasons the barrier betwixt this world and the invisible is according to their belief for the nonce partially withdrawn. There are hours also in each day and night when the seen and the unseen may meet and to a certain extent mingle. These hours are termed *yama*. Cynthia had experience of these demon-haunted hours. For instance, when the cook returning intoxicated from a commission on which he had been sent at mid-day, he had laid the blame on a "demon" that had "possessed" him when out at that "demon-haunted" hour:

Again when a *podyan* (Sinhalese house-boy) stole an ear-ring the defence he set up was that no respectable servant should be made to dust at that untimely hour when bad demons are lurking about on mischief bent: *he* didn't steal the ear-ring, the "bad demon" did. Moreover it was the lady's own fault, therefore she could not blame the *podyan*. A somewhat trying philosophy to accept. But meanwhile the bull-hackery went jogging along the dusty moonlit road, bearing Cynthia and her husband to the *Yakkadura*. An hour thus brought them to an open space in the midst of a cocoanut wood by the seashore. The first thing Cynthia remarked were the altars —five in number, specially erected and elaborate in construction—real works of art, all of them. On each was a goodly supply of fruit, flowers, and edibles, mangoes, plantains, papois, custard apples, with the blossoms of the orange, myrtle, areca and *ratmal*, rice and curried vegetables—offerings to that particular demon to whom that particular altar was dedicated. The space was corded in, the only individual at present within the sacred precincts being the *Kattadiya*, the devil priest or charmer.

For a Sinhalese a singularly fine man was he, the *Kattadiya*, deep-chested, muscular and tall. His only garment was a loincloth, a garland of *garulla* leaves adorning his waist as well as his brow. His dark eyes shone out from his haggard face and seemed literally to blaze forth magnetism. There was no superfluous flesh on his well-knit form. A statue of Hermes in bronze he might have passed for. In those eyes one found intelligence, dominating intelligence, besides the physical magnetism his whole personality seemingly gave out. In his right hand he held a rod called a *dhorjee*, said also to be charged with abundance of magnetism.

"A hypnotist," whispered Cynthia, "a powerful one too."

After they were seated—there were only two chairs for the Europeans' accommodation—a gun was fired to signify the ceremony would now commence. The reverberation echoed and thrilled the broad expanse of the moonlit Indian Ocean.

This particular ceremony or *Sanni Yakun Neteena* was for the purpose of dispossessing a certain Sinhalese woman into whom an evil demon was said to have entered.

The story went that this woman being compelled to go to a well which was a well-known haunt of evil demons, particularly at *Yama* hours, fell a victim to obsession—became in fact a *Taincama*, as the natives say, or "made solitary." Since that evil hour her entire nature had changed, they affirmed. She had neglected her domestic duties—she who had formerly been an exemplary housewife, of late had taken to wander in graveyards (*sohona*) "along with the demons," existing on roots, snails, and toads, and behaving generally in a "shameless way," report went on. Her relatives being scandalised by such conduct, and being also well to do, had secured the services of a first class devil charmer (*Kattadiya*), who had the reputation of being unfailing in his endeavours. The woman herself was present, shut up in a *cadjan* fisher-hut lent for the occasion, but at request Cynthia was granted permission to see her in her sad and awful condition. Sad and awful indeed that condition was! Scarcely human this woman looked, she who was as yet quite young in years and previous to this mishap, whatever it really was, had been renowned for her comeliness and good character. The poor creature made no response to Cynthia's expressions of sympathy; they fell on her hearing unheeded. Her human intelligence appeared to be frozen, while some other seemed certainly to obsess her; the light of a demon's eye surely shone in those wild and vicious orbs.

"Very bad demon this, Lady," said the man deputed to act guide. But this *Kattadiya* great man, he drive out bad demon, woman get well. Lady will see.

"Many demons coming help this one: this garden soon full. But no good. This *Kattadiya* drive all 'way. All get food, then at cock-crow all go 'way."

At this juncture a band struck up, a native band composed of tom-toms, reeds, viols, cymbals, pipes. This was the overture. The music symbolised the facts of the case, and was really so descriptive Cynthia could follow, from what she had previously been told, the course of the malady or affliction from which the erstwhile decent living village woman was suffering. It was easy to picture the simple creature going to the well for water, half reluctantly, for was she not aware that demons were on the lurk? The overture only lasted some quarter of an hour, but this sufficed for telling the whole story. Cynthia followed the realistic musical interpretation intently. At its conclusion *Netun Karayo* or devil-dancers came bounding into the charmed circle: literally charmed, for that rite of itself had been a ceremony performed beforehand. The dress of these *Netun Karayo* was fantastic in the extreme—what we should call accordian-pleated short skirts of brightest colours, with most hideous of masks and chains of wild blossoms. Others, instead of the masks, had their faces painted red and white *à la Européen*; while others again were encased in skins of the cheetah, leopard, jaguar, or jackal.

Whatever it was, the impersonation was well maintained. The dance was, like the overture, symbolic. Indeed, each movement, as each contortion of their lithe bodies, was full of meaning. Before each altar a different "figure" was "danced." It were better to say a mimic pantomime was enacted. Then in front of the hut wherein the *Taincama* was secluded, another "dance," outrivalling all the rest in frenzy. In response came from within a low savage growl.

"Lady hear bad devil?" asked the *cicerone*.

All this was accomplished with lightning rapidity. A gong was then sounded, whose reverberations seemed to shake not only the coast but the calm moonlit ocean. Simultaneously dance and music ceased. Not a leaf rustled, not a whisper broke the sudden death-like silence. Then the *Kattadiya*, with a wave of his *dhorjee*, commenced. In a nasal yet powerful monotone pages and pages of *mantras* were recited—exhortations, supplications, demands. At the name of each god or demon the garulla-garlanded head bowed, and the *dhorjee* was made to make a mystic sign or symbol in mid-air. The clear

Photo. Platé, Ceylon

NETUN KAREWAYO, DEVIL-DANCERS, AND BEREWAYO, TOM-TOM-BEATERS REHEARSING IN A COCOANUT-WOOD FOR A YAKKADURA, DEVIL-DANCE

enunciation might have been heard for miles in that silent tropical night. Almost in the centre the priest stood, although his majestic figure turned slightly to that altar whose presiding deity (demon) he addressed, while clouds of incense arose from brazen braziers, upon whose embers handfuls of fresh resin and incense and other narcotics were continually being thrown.

Alternately this continued—the *Netun Karayo* and their "dances"; the *Kattadiya* and his *mantras*—until nearly midnight. Then came an interval, in which the priest sought rest and refreshment, taking a bath in the sea and changing his clothes—as much as there was to change. What became of the "dancers" Cynthia knew not. They dispersed. The spectators strolled about chewing "betel" and drinking king cocoanut water, so that the only sounds from the Europeans' vantage was the lap, lap of white wavelets on the sandy beach, and the distant roar of breakers away on the coral reefs.

But on the stroke of midnight all reassembled. And now came the *pièce de résistance.* The woman for whose sake this *Sanni Yakun Neteena* was held was now released from seclusion. Defiantly she wrenched herself free from the hand that released her. Savagely she glared around at each and all until her wild eyes fell on those of the *Kattadiya.* Gradually those of the woman were transfixed.

The wildness faded in them; a somnolent, sightless look took its place. Having pinioned her gaze thus, the *Kattadiya* commenced making circles in the air with his *dhorjee*. These circles he willed her gaze should follow. Even as the *dhorjee* went round, so did the woman's eyes follow, the circles widening until it was incumbent on her head, her bust to the waist, to move with the rotations. Faster and faster also became these gyrations, so that the form, which previously had been of cataleptic rigidity, relaxed, grew supple and—*obedient*. And now a smile, a very faint smile, passed over the devil-priest's impassive countenance. Suddenly the uplifted hand stopped, with the wand raised high. The woman's eyes fixed themselves on it in a glazed and seemingly sightless stare. Then the *Kattadiya*, stooping, blew upon them. The vacant stare instantaneously gave place to intelligence, scarcely of a normal or human order yet though. Pointing the *dhorjee* in the direction of the fisher-hut, the priest then willed his patient to return. Slowly she obeyed that will, reluctant still.

Now wild shouts and yells heralded the return of the *Netun Karayo*, the *Kattadiya* retiring with beads of perspiration on his brow. To *will* in such a way is to part with one's very life. After much the same had occurred again in the way of dancing, the priest returned. And now came the *grand coup.* Extending his long and brawny brown arms, with fingers pointing directly at the *cadjan* hut, his lustrous magnetic eyes looking out weirdly through the smoke of incense, a dead silence was maintained. The audience waited in breathless expectancy—waited for long, it seemed, though it might probably have been but a few minutes. Then there was a rustle. Following that came the *Taincama* from out the hut, her eyes again wild and resentful. Mechanically she moved, as though drawn or propelled, moreover against her own desire and will. A step, and then another, and another; her wild eyes fixed on the *Kattadiya* half defiantly. So on, like an unaccustomed automaton until close—close beneath the *Kattadiya's* gaze.

Again the priest blew of his breath upon her—on her eyes, her brow. And presently a long, low sigh, terminating in a shrill, ear-splitting shriek that rent the heavy atmosphere and died away far over the ocean, and the woman sank on the ground at the *Kattadiya's* feet. The victory was accomplished. The demon was exorcised. The woman a *Taincama* no more. At a glance from the priest two of her relatives came forward and bore her insensible body away into the hut to be anointed and clothed in new white garments. Consciousness presently returned, and the woman now looked and appeared to be her normal self.

The first cock crew when she opened her eyes, seemingly awaking from a bad dream. A shudder passed through her frame; then she smiled—a smile of relief. Cynthia asked if she were well and happy, and the answer was: "Oh yes, lady; so well, so happy. Only a little tired, and wanting to get home to my children." Then a gun was fired, and the magpie proclaimed the first glimmer of the dawn.

CHAPTER V

Cynthia's best gown—Its fate—An Indian *Dhurzee* —King Solomon, nothing less — Moti's delight— East *versus* West—Moti could and Moti *did.*

"WHY not give it to a *dhurzee?*" some one said, referring to a precious *crèpe-de-chine* gown, the pet of Cynthia's trousseau, that only needed skilful handling to create of it "a dream."

"A *dhurzee!*" Cynthia had not been long out in Ceylon *urgo* the shriek, "My ex-*quisite crèpe-de-chine?*"

"Oh, but these *dhurzees* are geniuses, I can assure you," said the lady friend. "That last habit of mine fits to perfection. I *never* send home for my things now, and *rarely* pay through the nose at the European stores out here. Try a *dhurzee—do.*" Now the lady adviser was herself a fashion-plate materialised, perfectly patterned say for church parade at the height of the London season. The fact of this being Colombo, with the thermometer at 100 degrees in the shade, was a detail to a leader of colonial *beau monde*—an up-to-date English woman of fashion.

'I'll give you the address of a tip-top man—works for her Excellency. Try him, and you'll declare him a Redfern—a Worth."

Cynthia sent off a "chit" there and then: "Come to-morrow morning," addressed to *N. Tamberaninyi-Pillai, Dhurzee Street.*

To-morrow morning came and went without the shadow of a *dhurzee*, likewise other to-morrow mornings.

"Oh, that's nothing. The custom of the country: a little way they have," observed Cynthia's friend. "*He'll* turn up."

And he did—when least expected—when well-nigh given up, in fact.

At sight of his commanding figure coming up the compound, Cynthia was reminded of some scriptural personage of illustrious degree. A striking figure that inspired respect—reverence indeed—a figure that seemed to radiate a sort of sacred importance. Such was *N. Tamberaninyi Pillai.*

Appoo, *Ayah*, *Podyan*, all were set about making preparations. Meanwhile, after a *salaam* to the *Memsahib* (for the *dhurzee*, of course, is always Hindoo), *N. Tamberaninyi Pillai* walked with the grace and dignity of a prince—in a fairy tale—towards the regions where curry and rice is always *en evidence.* When all was ready, *N. Tamberaninyi Pillai* emerged at the summons of the *Appoo*. The *Ayah—Moti* stood at an angle, her much beringed finger in her mouth, her black eyes aglow on what might be termed his Serene Presence.

"Now, *Dhurzee*," said Cynthia, nerving herself up to the occasion, "now, *Dhurzee*, I want you to make me an evening gown just like this," producing a fashion-plate from a recent issue of a London lady's paper.

"This is the material—very beautiful, is it not? Well, I want you to cut it so that nothing is wasted. The material——"

"*Salaam*, lady—*cloth*." There was a politely corrective tone in the Indian's soft voice.

"Well, cloth, if you like. *We* say material. Ahem! Now, the skirt must of course be the latest, and the *corsage* perfect in fit. To insure this I've had the pattern sent out. All you have to do is to—well, be *very* particular and—and—" Cynthia meant to add "follow my instructions," but a pair of eyes, dark lustrous, deep—deeper than that well wherein truth is said to dwell—eyes with a power and a mystery in them *no* European can or ever will fathom, much less solve—such a pair of orbs was upon her, and Cynthia's power of speech was paralysed. Then the *Dhurzee* spoke.

"Lady making lady's evening gown or *Dhurzee?*" Cynthia, dropping her regards, commenced to smooth out the *crèpe-de-chine* and tittered. She returned to the charge in a second or two, however, with a cough. " Ahem! Now, *Dhurzee* "—Cynthia prided herself on her softly persuasive tone at times: an Irishman once told her it would coax the stripe off a jackass's back—" Now, *Dhurzee*, here is the table. I had it brought out on to the back verandah. Let us begin. Table, scissors, tape-measure, all are here at hand for you. But—ah! Perhaps you'd best begin by taking my measure" (Cynthia little realised *that* had already been done—figuratively), saying which she turned and turned herself about, hands on hips, in order to show off her slim figure at its best. " Now," when the pose was perfect. " But," went on Cynthia, " I ought to tell you first, I always prefer—*Ayah? Ayah?*" Glancing over her shoulder, Cynthia beheld *Dhurzee* and *Ayah* in close confab over " chews of betel." " *Ayah?* "

" Yes, lady, I coming—'mediately."

" I want you to hold the pins, paper, pencil, &c., while the *Dhurzee* takes my measure, and I want the *Dhurzee*——"

But a pair of bronze-brown hands were now uplifted to a hieroglyphiced brow, and a majestic head bent while a sonorous voice said:

" *Salaam!* " The same bronze hands then proceeded to pick up the muslin *Kambaya*, preparatory to treading the dust. Then a right regal back was turned, and the right regal owner trod the steps of the back verandah in righteous indignation.

"*Dhurzee? Ayah?* What *is* the meaning of this?"

Moti, the Ayah, pouting her *betel*-stained lips, stepped forward and said something in Tamil to the August Presence, who, after a brief while, returned to the verandah with an air of infinite condescension.

Cynthia could not—being sensitive to outward impressions—but remark, and, yes, admire the bearing and manner of this lordly figure of a man, the bearing rather of one of those chieftains of old, endowed by nature or inheritance with that native dignity combined with grace no amount of instruction, much less affectation, can impart. And yet this *Dhurzee* was by profession—if tailoring be a profession—but the proverbial ninth part of a man!

"*Dhurzee* saying, Lady," vouchsafed Moti, "who know tailor-make-work best—*Dhurzee* or Lady?"

Now, as the answer to this question, even in its as yet unproven state, admitted of little doubt, if any, Cynthia deemed it prudent to reply with an amicable titter, and murmur something about his serene highness having his own way. Forthwith the scissors, the *Dhurzee's* own, and mostly resembling a pair of shears, were leisurely taken by one of the bronze-brown hands, while the other laid hold of the *crèpe-de-chine en masse* and dumped the same down on the cement floor. Cynthia's heart leaped. Then the shears-like scissors coursed the silken material at a canter. And all the while a pair of unfathomable black eyes retained a devouring gaze on Cynthia. Five feet seven and three quarters—her full length; up and down those black eyes went, taking in apparently every curve, every crease. Cynthia's heart, after that one leap, stood still. Power of speech was paralysed too. Her exquisite *crèpe-de-chine* — mutilated — spoilt! Little wonder she was stunned. Only when Moti spoke did Cynthia gather herself together, so to speak.

"*Dhurzee* saying, 'Lady please go 'way.' *Dhurzee* not wanting lady more."

A long, long breath was Cynthia's. Was it a sigh? as with a last look at her *crèpe-de-chine* prone in length, she turned and went away—back into the bungalow, to the piano, where she sought distraction, oblivion, anything in Wagnerian excitement on the piano. But no, the *Götterdämmerung* even failed. Her mind was beset with the awful agony of the utter destruction of her best evening gown. Fain would she have dashed back to the back verandah and demanded the material—the "cloth," as this murderous *Dhurzee* called it, but a voice within said, "Wait." Oh, it was hard to obey! The trials of Tantalus were nothing to this. Crash! came her hands down on the ivory keys.

"I'll do the accounts. *Appoo*, send the cook." Cynthia was a great believer in counter-irritants. Account-taking is one of a European housekeeper's utter human miseries in Ceylon. Cook came. An argument speedily ensued. The native is possessed of a special faculty whereby two and two are made five. His subtlety of argument, moreover, in explaining the why and wherefore is incontrovertible. Cynthia was soon involved. And whilst in this maze—this labyrinth of metaphysics—her *crèpe-de-chine* was forgotten—for the time.

"This something 'ceptional, Lady," explained Cook, entering upon a compound complication of reasoning whereby he sought to prove he had given seventy-five cents for a chicken when in reality he had only given fifty. Cynthia was fanning herself furiously, notwithstanding the fact of the punkah overhead, and trying her level best to follow the intricacies of the other side of the dispute when the Ayah came in.

"*Dhurzee* saying Lady, please come see." Cynthia was up in a moment. A hand gripped her heart. "Er—well, don't give so much again: I'm sure it's not worth it" to the Cook, who beamed and salaamed. Then there came a flutter at her heart, and after that calm—dead calm. "Spoilt, of course—ah, well!" And on she went to the back verandah, with the numbness of resignation.

There was the *Dhurzee*, serenely chewing betel, the *crèpe-de-chine* still on the ground, only that now it presented the appearance of a prostrate ghost, in *form* bearing an uncomfortable resemblance to herself.

Moti, advancing, picked it up.

"*Dhurzee* saying Lady please try on."

Cynthia, turning, motioned the *Ayah* towards her dressing-room.

"Skirtie coming first, Lady." Then in a minute or two, "Heigh-ho! Skirtie fitting good—*very* good." Moti's black orbs rolled with delight. "That *Dhurzee* good, Lady—damn good—no?"

"Hush! Yes, it seems to fit," Cynthia turned herself this way and that before the cheval glass. "Yes, the *skirt* seems all right. Now for the bodice. Be careful, it's only tacked."

"Heigh-ho!" Moti clapped her hands and commenced capering about the room.

"Lady looking like picture in European reading-book. That *Dhurzee* good, Lady thinking—not?"

"Yes. Well, really, it—it's excellent—so far,"

said Cynthia, still revolving before the mirror. Then. "*Dhurzee?*"

No need was there to call. The *Dhurzee* was there, at the door: natives have no notion of the sacredness of privacy.

"Oh, you're there. Well, *Dhurzee*, it's very good indeed. I do hope you won't spoil it—" continuing turning this way and that before the glass.

"*Lady!!!*"

Cynthia laughed pleasantly, she *felt* those eyes upon her—"I mean—it's really *so* excellent I hope, I *do* hope——"

"What's he saying, Moti?"

"*Dhurzee* saying Lady give now five rupees, *Dhurzee* bring back dress in two three day."

"Oh yes, he shall have five rupees—on account."

"And, please let me have it back in *three* days at the most. I'm wanting it, and—I'm sure he'll make an exquisite gown of it, tell him. Here is the five rupees."

Had he asked for double that amount it is probable he would have got it. The relief after the agony of direful anticipation, fear, dread, horror, was delightful.

"*Dhurzee* saying *Salaam*, Lady. Dress he bringing back finished three day."

With this exit *Dhurzee*, also *Ayah*.

Ten minutes later, when Cynthia rang for Moti, after a third summons the *Appoo* appeared.

"Ayah not nowhere, Lady," said he.

"Oh, very well, I'll manage. All the same she shouldn't have gone out without permission." That entire day passed without Moti's reappearance. So did next day and next, and next, when the new evening-gown was to be brought home by the *Dhurzee*.

Alas! day No. 3 came and went. No gown, no *Dhurzee*, no *Ayah*. It was strange, to say the least of it. Cynthia trusted no harm had happened, nothing serious had occurred. Cynthia's husband smiled. So also did the rest of the servants.

A post-card was sent to *N. Tamberaninyi Pillai.* No response. A telegram. No response. Then the *Appoo* with a "chit." The *Appoo* returned, not that day but next, at daybreak.

"*N. Tamberaninyi Pillai* gone," said he.

"Gone?" echoed Cynthia aghast. Gone *where?* The *Appoo* shook his head.

"I'll go myself. Tell the *Muttu* to harness the horse and bring the buggy—at once."

Within a quarter of an hour Cynthia was *en route* to *Dhurzee* Street. Once arrived at No. 9, Cynthia descending found herself the centre of a crowd of *Dhurzees*.

"Lady wanting *Dhurzee?* I come Lady's

'MOTI COULD, AND MOTI DID'

house. I good testimonials got: King's House Governor's Lady I work. See, testimonials, Lady," and a babel of tongues and a forest of bare brown arms encompassed her.

"Hush! hush! I want *N. Tamberaninyi Pillai*."

At the mention of this name much chattering went on in Tamil, all double-Dutch to Cynthia. "Where is he? I want to see him. I *must* see him." She had been long enough out in Ceylon to know the importance of the imperative. "Bring him."

"*N. Tamberaninyi Pillai* not here. That *dhurzee* gone 'way home India, Lady, "week more 'go." Cynthia's heart sank and turned to stone.

"And — my evening-gown? — and — Moti?"

"Lady evening-gown, good gown Moti liking much, go too, Moti go too—all go India, not come back—never 'gain."

Thus perished Cynthia's hopes, pride, all. "My *lovely crèpe-de-chine*—oh!"

"Moti! Moti! how *could* you?"

But Moti could—and Moti *did*.

CHAPTER VI

Cynthia on the verandah surrounded by her pets—Happy days—Who flourish best in the First Crown Colony?—Punch and his prejudices —"European not like dirt"—The Colombo Municipality—One of its "customs"—Another violation—In perilous proximity with an invading cobra — Cynthia's admiration —A picture in the sunlight—Punch to the rescue.

THOSE were happy days for Cynthia, seated at her writing-table on the verandah, with her faithful terrier *Punch* on guard, *Chin-Chin*, a pet turkey, as near as *Punch* permitted, and *Chou-Chou*, a *minah*, chattering a polyglot of English, Sinhalese, and Tamil, to the amazement of the passengers passing by in the *gharries*. These were her companions. But the nearest always, as well as the dearest, was *Punch*. Now *Punch*, begotten of *Judy*, was the "ugly duckling" of a brood of seven. Applications in plenty came for his brethren, none for himself.

"That dog only good for kill rats, plenty in kitchen," was the verdict of the Indian cook. "Master, let me take that dog on back verandah, never I let go in bungalow, I say d——n, good English." This graceful finish to the asseveration was intended to lend solemnity, and was accepted in that sense. One cannot be always moralising or didactic with a thermometer at 100 in the shade.

So it was that *Punch*, ugly *Punch's* life was spared. *Punch* certainly was ugly, comically ugly. One ear larger than the other and set more aft, eyes sharp and penetrating, but aslant; jaw underhung, betokening bull blood in his mongrel veins, and a tail everything it shouldn't be; a canine specimen made up of odd bits. Such was *Punch*, whose brethren were beauties.

Nobody wanted *Punch*—nobody. Now whether it was he experienced the same "cold shoulder" treatment from his kith and kin, Cynthia couldn't say, only that on the very day his eyes opened on this wicked world, when seated at tiffin she felt something move, and quickly snatching up her skirts in fear of a cobra discovered—the "ugly duckling." Such a comical twinkle came into his little beadlike eyes on meeting her own that she named him *Punch* there and then. How he had tumbled so far the canine deity alone knows! Why he should tumble to *her*, mystified her wildest imaginings!

"Why did you allow that dog to come into the bungalow?" questioned Cynthia's husband.

"Sar, I not allow: I not know dog coming."

"Take it away."

"*Salaam*, sar," and Punch was restored to the bosom of his family.

Next day the same occurred. Nobody saw him come, nevertheless there he was. Next day and the next. Cynthia, however, entered her protest against his being locked up at meal-times. Truth to tell, in her inner consciousness there lurked an idea, a superstition some would say. Already she was proving the truth of the bird of Paradise, this land was not all Eden. "Keep him; he will be your *mascotte;* he will bring you luck," spake that idea within. *Punch* might be *bizarre*, but he had character; indomitability worthy of Bismarck was in that jaw; sincerity, devotion, illumined those little slant eyes. To herself Cynthia said "yes, and *soul*." What would Mrs. Colonial Grundy say to that? What *more* rather than she and her votaries—all in sure possession of their passports to heaven, *via les convenances*—were already saying of "such extraordinary conduct in a European *lady*, exercising her brains, or—having brains at all!" When his little limbs grew stronger, one day in desperation *Punch* made a frantic effort to jump into the Stanhope phaeton and take his seat beside his mistress. He would have fallen, perhaps have broken his back or a limb, had not Cynthia seized him. The horse, a high-mettled Australian, fearing something irregular, leapt, bounded and galloped off at a furious pace. *Punch* was victorious; he kept his place at his mistress's feet. Another day a *rickshaw*, containing a European helplessly intoxicated, ran over him. *Punch* on foot, following his mistress in the phaeton, emerged unharmed, although the *rickshaw* was capsized. A volley of foul abuse was hurled at *Punch's* heels, to be followed by a brick, when Cynthia, pulling up, sprang out and confronted the angered "angel in embryo" with a look in her eyes before which that "angel" quailed and let drop the brick. *Punch* himself was no saint—he didn't pretend to be. He had deadly animosities, and was a prime hater. The category of his aversion comprised natives, beggars, postmen, sneaks and cowards (animal and human), snobs, and swagger; all of which flourish in His Majesty's First Crown Colony.

"What do you think of *that?*" asked his expressive little eyes, when something cruel in "mushroom" grandeur or crude style passed by. Bad form he could not endure, nor vulgar taste.

Gradually *Punch* outgrew his ugliness; not so his comicality. He was the incarnation of the comic; no high and mighty human being ever had a keener sense of it. Nothing amused him more than to terrify the Sinhalese, who are the greatest cowards on earth. Afterwards, he would look round at his mistress and laugh—yes, laugh. It was only pretence on his part. But when a man seized a naked child and held as a shield of protection before him, *Punch* waxed serious and *really* furious. *Punch* likewise had what might be termed "holy horrors," one of them being uncleanliness, another drunkenness. Nothing savoury would tempt him to eat off a dirty plate, no matter how hungry he might be. One morning on their return from the matutinal canter, both very hungry, *Punch* made a dash for his breakfast awaiting him. To Cynthia's surprise, however, he returned, looking up in her face and "whee-wheeing" pleadingly. Then, as she went on sipping her tea—for Cynthia's was only *chota hazira*—and fanning herself, he began tugging at her riding skirt, and looking back in the direction of his curry and rice.

"What *is* the matter, Punchie?" asked his mistress.

"Very well, I'll go and see." Meanwhile, the "dog-boy" coming up, said:

"*Punch* not eat to-day, Lady—Friday. No good dog eat Friday—*Christian* dog."

"Rubbish! dogs eat on Friday the same as other days," was the reply, as Cynthia gathered up her skirts to *Punch's* apparent delight.

There stood the dog-plate of good food untouched; around the rim, though, were dirty thumb-marks. This the reason why *Punch* had refused to eat. The plate being changed he went at the food vigorously, but not without showing his thanks to his mistress first.

"That dog, European, Lady, not like dirt," was the dog-boy's comment.

Another time when they had been obliged to change their cook, afternoon tea not being forthcoming notwithstanding orders, and no explanation being vouchsafed by the *Appoo*, Cynthia, having become reckless by now concerning the "customs of the country," went herself to see the reason why. There lay the new cook in a deep sleep on the kitchen floor, so deep he made no response to his name. *Punch* walked round him taking stock, then growled rather ferociously. At this the man opened his eyes, looked fearfully at the dog, then fell back helplessly, with an entreating look in his eyes, and in a low tone murmured, "Fever—fever, lady."

Now, as there wasn't the slightest smell of arrack about, Cynthia believed it.

"Never mind; don't disturb yourself. I'll make the tea with my kettle and send you some quinine and ice. Hush, *Punch!*" for *Punch* was working himself up into a fury and bade fair to tear the poor man's clothes, if not the poor man himself, to pieces. "Come away!"

But instead of obeying, Punch's fury waxed, and fearing something serious might occur Cynthia turned back, to find the invalid had risen, and although supported by the wall, his attitude was menacing, tragic, as he brandished a long knife, his eyes aflame with anger. In a flash Cynthia realised the fact. The man was under the influence of *bhang*, and had "*run amuck !*"

As soon as she turned, the man's attention was given from the dog to herself. Staggering and uttering wild words in Tamil, he made for Cynthia with one hand, the knife gleaming in the other. Cynthia was within an ace of his grasp when *Punch* with a bound, springing into the air some five feet or more, caught the man's *nainsook* sleeve in his teeth and tugging for all he was worth, tore it to shreds, but not before the knife fell to the ground. In an instant it was in *Punch*'s mouth. The man reeled back against the wall.

"*Appoo ! Ayah ! Muttu !*" cried Cynthia ; but not a servant responded to the call. They knew full well the condition of the man and what might accrue ; so each and all had found something to do at a safe distance. However, *Punch* was there, and it was owing to his presence probably that Cynthia's life was saved. Brave little fellow ! How he held on to that knife !

One afternoon Cynthia, seated on the verandah, awaited the phaeton to drive her and *Punch* to the *Secretariat*, as usual, for the "Master."

"It's four o'clock ; why doesn't the carriage come ?" she asked the *Appoo*.

The *Appoo*, smiling, shook his head. "I not know, lady."

"*Punch*, go and see." Cynthia had her suspicions. She had been long enough in Ceylon to have a stock of them, and no better detective was there than *Punch*. There was no deceiving *him*. His intelligent countenance, moreover, Cynthia read like an open book. *Punch* went—but did not return.

"*Punch! Punch! Punch!*" No response. Then the "dogboy" came in breathless haste from the back regions, gasping:

"Lady, *Punch* gone! Cart come take *Punch* away."

"What!" from Cynthia, aghast.

"Cart come and take *Punch*, lady," repeated the boy, his big eyes looking abnormally big now.

Cynthia was out in a flash. There in the high road was the Municipal dogcart, with a collection of vagrant dogs, amongst which was *Punch*, gazing in a dazed sort of way through the iron bars.

This sufficed. Cynthia was down the road and up to the cart in a trice, demanding her dog. The men in charge—as great villains as the Municipality could surely find—took no heed of her demand, but stated *their* demand, which being rejected, called forth impertinence. A constable standing at the corner was summoned, who entered into parley (and would-be partnership) with the municipal *employés*, with the only result that the demand on their side went up in value.

Meanwhile a crowd of native vagabonds collected. Cynthia dropped her fan. It was picked up in the toes of one and transferred by hand to his waist-pocket. The sun was scorching. The rascals, constable included, were implacable, while the cries of *Punch*, next to a mangy mongrel, were heartrending.

"Where are they being taken?" asked Cynthia.

"To the Town Hall--to be killed," was the reply of one in the crowd, a respectable-looking *Appoo*.

"To be killed!" echoed Cynthia. Then making what the Americans call "a stiff upper lip," Cynthia murmured below her breath, "*Will* they!"

Through the hosts of Europeans, natives, and burghers, all out for their evening drive, Cynthia picked her way—on foot. The phaeton was at the verandah on her return.

"Drive to the Town Hall, quick!" said she, taking her seat therein. Once there her request to see a European official met with a stare. Dauntless, Cynthia passed on up the stairs and entered the first room, spite of restraining tongues and hands. Herein was seated an elderly gentleman of the burgher class. Cynthia, bowing, addressed him, telling her tale, as her breeding and education dictated. Not only courtesy but sympathy did she receive. That kindly old gentleman, though not of her own nationality, was himself a lover of dogs, and assured her she should have her *Punch* as soon as he arrived. After twenty minutes' conversation, during which Cynthia got cool, a servant came and said the cart had returned. Another couple of minutes and *Punch* was on his mistress's lap, his little heart thumping with delight.

Thus then were the Municipal *employés* deprived of the *santosum* they anticipated when *stealing* Cynthia's pet *Punch*. They reckoned without Punch's mistress.

After this Punch was more devoted than ever. He would gaze up into Cynthia's face to read there the very secret of her soul. Not a shade on her brow escaped his notice, nor failed to call forth his tender sympathies. Ever responsive to inmost, subtlest feeling, no companion more desirable, no friend more staunch than he. When she put on a new hat, or blouse, or skirt he would, after inspection, signify his approval or disapproval by bounding and barking joyously around her, or by turning away with a shrug and a swagger. Once—it was at the seaside bungalow, Cynthia, feeling depressed, was stretched on a couch writing in pencil to her friend, an Austrian countess, to whom she confided all.

Punch, very quiet, she believed asleep, was beneath the couch. All at once he barked, a long low growl ending in a bark.

"Quiet, *Punch!*"

But Punch was not quiet, nor would be.

Cynthia, deeming it but one more of the many beggars come to the verandah, did not trouble to look up, until *Punch*, having come out from beneath the couch, jumped up and caught her sleeve to arrest her attention Then Cynthia raised her eyes. But even while she spoke reprovingly on the one side, on the other she beheld a cobra, coiled up on the floor, its head erect, its eyes gazing at her on a level with her own. Beyond the verandah the sun was setting in the deep Indian Ocean, its rays like golden gossamer ladders, stretching from that ruddy golden orb direct to her, and passing between through the scaly skin of the cobra. Every mark was shown upon the cobra's transparent skin, so that the figurings looked like hieroglyphics in gems. Indeed the whole creature seemed mythological rather than real, or a vision creature from the jewel-mines of *Golconda*. So beautiful, who *could* be afraid? Not Cynthia, although *Punch* might be—for *her* sake. May be it exercised a power of fascination over her, as the cobra is said to do. However it was, Cynthia gazed admiringly at it, its jewelled hood with the coronet, its scintillating, gem-like eyes, while *Punch* grew desperate. Failing in his efforts to draw his mistress away, he suddenly took a leap over the couch; then straightening his fore limbs, he planted himself fixedly by the side of the cobra, barking so that his body vibrated with the effort.

The cobra dooped its majestic head, turning sinuously this way and that to avoid the infuriated dog. Now that it was no longer under the golden rays of the setting sun it looked what it was—the snake, nothing more. Wriggling its slimy body, half in fear, half in retaliation, it crouched and sneaked along the floor, spitting out the virus in all directions as it went. Then was it Cynthia's turn to fear—for Punch. "Punch! Punchie! Come here," she cried. "Come here, *Punchie!*" But *Punchie* declined until he had driven the snake out on to the verandah, so that his mistress was safe. In answer to Cynthia's calls the servants appeared at the door opening on to the *back* verandah, but not a step further would any of them come until the cobra had disappeared. Then, "Lady not have cobra killed? Cobra bring lady good-luck," from the *Ayah*. "That cobra do lady no hurt—head keep up—always so when cobra friendly. I know that, so I not come quick," from the Hindoo cook, each and all ready to come in and gossip now. Human nature is much alike, black or white!

Alas! there came a day—but many chapters must intervene first. Cynthia would rather not anticipate the little mound at the foot of a cocoanut-palm at Mount Lavinia, where her little protector and friend lies sleeping, while she, his mistress, far away in England, often speaks, and still more often thinks, of him. Some day she may visit that grave, contrary to any "custom of the country," or of the orthodox belief that a dog is unworthy of a soul. Some day she hopes to—she believes she *shall*—meet Punch again.

CHAPTER VII

Another "custom of the country"—The *Muttu's* Dinner-party—An invitation for the *Durasani*—Cynthia's perplexity overcome by a bright idea—Nineteen fine fat rats.

CYNTHIA had by this time accustomed herself to write on the verandah for a couple of hours every morning. Her experiences were so interesting, surely they were worth recording. At any rate, such work as this was more congenial to her than giving herself up to the inanities of a very heterogeneous "society," although there *were* some who could and did understand and appreciate culture. Her experiences were not without a humorous side; humour always appealed to Cynthia, even though she might be a victim of it. One day she was much disturbed by voices proceeding from the region of the stables. More than once she had summoned the *Appoo* and told him to put a stop to it, without any satisfactory result however. "Oh! dear. I must go myself!" Cynthia sighed, for the thermometer marked 110 in the shade.

"*Muttu* got many friends there, lady, all talking together, angry—lady not going?" the *Appoo* vouchsafed as explanation, at last, when his mistress got up to go.

"Indeed I *will* go, and see what it means."

Now under the shade of *cadjan* the *Muttu* was still grooming the mare Cynthia had ridden that morning. At a distance was a huge *chattie* upon a roaring fire, while standing about and "talking all together," as the *Appoo* had said, were some six or seven women, "grass-women" as they are called, by reason of their bringing the daily rations of grass for the horses. Talking, gesticulating angrily, with intermittent appeals to the *Muttu*, who went on "massaging" the animal as only native grooms can, or at any rate, do. His back was turned, so that he was unaware of Cynthia's presence until she spoke.

"What is the meaning of this, *Muttu?* Who are these women, and why are they here? *That* is our grass-woman, and *that* one we discharged. Who are the others?"

The *Muttu* first *salaamed*, then hung his head, and although a faint smile lit up his good-looking face, Cynthia fancied she detected a deeper shade of red come over his ruddy-bronze skin. "Who *are* they?" she repeated.

"Er—ar—these women, grass-women, lady," was the reply as he helped himself to a "chew of betel." The women had fallen back, silenced. But only for a moment. One, a bold-eyed, handsome creature, came forward. The rest followed suit. Bare brown arms were held up supplicatingly, while the babel was resumed in a language of which Cynthia knew not one word.

"Hush! Stop them all talking at once, *Muttu*. What have they to say—to *me?*" she asked. "Who is this woman?" specifying the bold one.

"Er—that woman, lady? That woman my wife."

"But you told me your wife was dead. That is why I allow you to have your little motherless child here," said Cynthia, fanning herself furiously, for the sun was in mid-heaven and its rays beat down on her, spite of the shade.

"This one *new* wife, lady," replied the *Muttu*, commencing with the curry-comb.

"You didn't tell me you had married again. Well, and the rest?" Whether Cynthia's sweeping gesture with the fan were taken as an invitation to come forward or not, they did—in a body, though *not* unanimously. And their voices!

"Hush! Stop, for goodness' sake!" At this each woman turned on her neighbour, keeping her back, and sidling up nearer herself, while pointing at the others angrily, the bold "wife" first and foremost. Though all were quarrelsome, there was a sort of trade union against this one.

"Now, *Muttu*, I insist upon knowing what this

is all about. What is that one saying?" pointing her fan at one as a random shot.

The *Muttu* smirked and hung his head over the mare's glossy coat.

"Speak, man, or you leave our service, and I shall state the reason in your register-book." (All servants are registered in Ceylon.)

"Ar—eh—ar—*that* one, lady?" pointing with the curry-comb. "That one saying *she* my wife," he went on, putting a finishing touch to the glossy coat, so that his back was towards his mistress.

"Humph! Another wife. Then, *that* one?" asked Cynthia, assuming a severe—a very severe tone.

"Er—*that* one? She saying *she* my wife," was the reply, helping himself to more *betel*.

Again the arms were outstretched. Again the clamour.

Meanwhile the pot began to boil. The "bold" one went to attend to it. The rest followed, bent on the same purpose, and a fierce altercation ensued.

"I will not have this going on in the compound. How *dare* they? They have no business here at all. What have they come for?"

The steaming fumes from the *chattie*, although very savoury, were somewhat overpowering in the terrific heat, the roaring fire as well.

"My wife come dine with me to-day, lady.

Very good dinner got. Other wife and other hear about good dinner, all come, then quarrel. I not like quarrel, lady, but how help? Low caste, these grass-women, no good, lady—I take other wife, better caste—no quarrels make. I——"

"Silence! You've said enough. It's—*disgraceful.*"

Cynthia was bewildered and perplexed. What *should* she do? All the other servants were by this time gathered round; all were on the broad grin. Certainly when one ventures to tamper with the "customs of the country" in the East one is likely to find oneself in a quandary. One of the women held an infant dangling on her hip. A ray of inspiration came to Cynthia as her eye alighted on the child.

"Whose child is this?" she asked, drawing herself up to her full height and dignity.

The *Muttu salaamed*, smiled, and said:

"My child that, lady," very proudly.

"Very well, then, this one, the mother, is your wife. Send the others away, and *never*—let—me—see—them—or have to speak about it again."

This was delivered in severe, very severe, tones indeed, and Cynthia, maintaining her full height and dignity, was turning when the *Muttu* spoke:

"Very good, lady. I send all 'way. But,

no good dinner give first? Lady see, good dinner!"

The lid was taken off, and indeed the fumes *were* appetising. Cynthia feared for their own 8 P.M. dinner being docked of its joint or poultry.

"What is it? Where did you get it?" she asked in breathless anxiety.

"Rats! Nineteen I catch—fat, big rats. Lady like taste?" But the "lady" had gone—with a shriek.

CHAPTER VIII

An expedition into the jungle—To travel *à la* gipsy—A Bohemian gipsy's prediction to be fulfilled—How the Sinhalese drive—What about the R.S.C.P.A. in Ceylon?—Putting up at an *Ambalama* (rest-house)—A tea-planter tells an amusing story—The footprint on Adam's Peak, and what came of it.

IT is very trying to a European constitution to live long in Colombo, even in the Cinnamon Gardens, the Hyde Park of Ceylon, where the roads are broad and the large winding lake, thanks to the Dutch, permits the sea breeze beyond to enter the spacious and picturesque bungalows. One may go to the hills truly, if one be fortunate enough to know somebody to leave in charge of the home, otherwise one is sure to be apprised of burglary, on a wholesale scale, for they who, at midday, when the family are taking their *siesta*, can make off with a dining-table which took their fancy must be experts in the profession, as indeed the Sinhalese are.

Cynthia became more and more anæmic every day. Nothing for it but a change to a cooler climate. Now it happened they had recently purchased a tract of land in the interior, for the purpose of planting. The accounts rendered by the man in charge—a Sinhalese—didn't appear to Cynthia very satisfactory, taking into consideration customs of the country notwithstanding. Meditating, she thought how practical as well as delightful it would be to go themselves.

"Impossible! for a lady, at any rate," was the reply to her suggestion. As if there were such a word in her vocabulary! As was the rule, however, she had her way. The anticipation of a time spent in the jungle away from all conventionality, all civilisation in fact, seemed to go far towards realising the wild dreams (or one of them) of her youth. Besides, had not a Bohemian gipsy once told her that she would travel "like the gipsy," in a far distant land, across the deep ocean? She recollected how her heart had bounded at the idea that day in the castle of her friend—the Austrian Countess. But—was it possible? She had been incredulous then. Was the prophecy indeed to be fulfilled in Ceylon?

From Colombo they were to travel by the early morning train to *Polghawehlaya*; the Indian cook with a goodly store of provisions, cooking utensils, Bass and Burgundy, accompanying. There they would be met by the superintendent of the estate with a cadjan covered double-bullock cart, and a couple of coolies. When the day came the heat was intense, notwithstanding the early hour. The country, excepting for the rivers, with their drooping willows and feathery bamboos, was flat and uninteresting. They were glad when they reached *Polghawelahaya.* Here was the superintendent, a well-groomed man of *Vellalah* caste, with the cart and coolies awaiting under the shade of the tamarinds. Cynthia was not prepossessed, spite of the man's appearance, which was everything that could be desired, save that he limped. Concerning this limp he had a tale to tell, which he forthwith commenced, while coolies, cook, all the rest worked away at unpacking, suspending the cooking utensils outside the cart, gipsy-fashion, and getting ready for travelling. The tale was lengthy, and reflected great credit on the narrator, the hero, in fact, who in his courageous endeavours to save his master's property had been savagely gored by a ferocious wild boar. Hence his lameness. Naturally this exempted him from work; likewise from walking; so that while the others took turns to rest, Jacobis retained his seat at the back of the cart in a state of supreme ease. It is marvellous how comfortable a native *can* make himself under conditions which to a European of the lowest class would be unendurable: Nature's merciful law of compensation. Under any circumstances, a seat in the cart was no bed of roses, as the bullocks, hardy little beasts the size of small donkeys, were given to making unexpected dashes in the direction of the side ditches, when over would go cart, crockery, contents human and otherwise, without and within, precipitating driver and passengers, together with the terrified delinquents, into the mud below. When, bruised and soiled, they extricated themselves and belongings, it demanded all their united efforts to right the cart—Jacobis always excepted. This little diversion occurred too frequently to possess the charm of novelty. Moreover, it was direfully provocative of prickly heat. A coolie was told off to walk by the side of each bull to endeavour to keep it in the straight and decidedly narrow way. But even their native vigilance was escaped at times.

The driver who sat asquat a bar connecting the shafts in front, had a habit Cynthia approved not of. On the haunches of each bull was a bad wound, inflicted purposely. Into this wound a stick was thrust, probing the festering flesh to the bone. If this sufficed not to set the poor creatures off, a knot was made in the tail, and bitten with all the might of the natives' elephantine "ivories." This is the Sinhalese method of driving. What of the R.S.P.C.A. in our First Crown Colony? Cynthia had frequently to ask this question. But being but a "writer for news-

Photo. Plate, Ceylon

DOUBLE-BULLOCK-CART WHICH SERVED AS THE GIPSY-CARAVAN

papers" as the "ladies" there put it, she got no reply.

The huge tamarind and mahogany trees made grateful shade for halting, whilst the cook prepared a capital tiffin or "afternoon tea." Really the Indian cook is a treasure—when sober. It is marvellous what a first-rate repast he can turn out from limited material and conveniences. The larder was well replenished by the produce of the gun—snipe, woodcock, jungle fowl, hare, &c., while chickens, the size of pigeons, with green bones and brunette skin, very good all the same, were purchasable, as also was buffalo's milk (which may be likened unto tepid water stirred up with a tallow candle). This so long as they passed through the villages.

The first night was comfortable enough, being spent at a Rest House, an *Ambalama* provided by Government for travellers, like the *dâk* bungalows of India. As they had wired beforehand a good dinner was in readiness, or supper, it might better be called, as they did not arrive until 10 P.M. The moon was increasing, and it was as light at night as an average sunless day in London.

Another European was quartered there, who, for want of something to do, was seeking to drown his *ennui*, in whisky and soda—another custom of the country. After supper, to which they did full justice, all adjourned to the verandah to enjoy the moonlight, a chat and a *W. and S.*

"You'll break your back riding in that cart," said the new acquaintance. "Psha! adventures! not worth it out here! I've been out planting eighteen years, and know no more of the Island than up and down, to and from my place and Colombo—with a little Kandy and Nuraliya thrown in. 'Tisn't worth it. It's hard luck at best, tea planting nowadays—unless something unexpected turns up. Here's an experience of a chap I know?"

He then commenced a story which Cynthia thought afterwards worth taking notes of, with the following result.

The Planter's Story

"It's rough on you, old man, but buck up, there's a turn to every tide. Whatever you do, don't take too much quinine. I know a man in the 90th who's gone stone deaf through it, dosing himself eternally for malaria in some God-forsaken station. I'll look in in a day or too. Meanwhile, buck up, I say."

Saying which Dick Berkeley, as he was always called, mounted his *tat* and galloped away.

It *was* "rough" on Forster. Ever since he came out to Ceylon he had had bad luck. And that was five years ago. After serving his time as a "creeper" on a tea estate (or garden as they say out there), which means all work and no pay, work from day-dawn till night under a scorching sun, he had got a berth as assistant superintendent, whose only difference consisted in having to bear the brunt of anxiety and responsibility, and to endeavour to keep himself on a stipend which makes a bottle of Bass at a rupee an undreamt-of luxury, and all other creature comforts wraiths of bygone days. Then, when fortune seemed to smile upon him in getting a superintendentship, the property passed into other hands, who made different arrangements; and now, when about to get a post that promised pretty well, he was stricken with a bad attack of malaria and some one else put in. His friend had not had altogether plain-sailing himself, consequently he was able to sympathise with Forster, and did heartily, as only men (with all their shortcomings) do.

"Anything I can do, old man—practical, you understand," patting his pocket, "shall be delighted," he had said before mounting his pony—a hardy little beast. And Forster knew right well he meant it.

"It's this confounded fever that humps a fellow so," was the reply—perhaps an apology for the moistening of his eye. A couple of days later a *bearer* came with a note, and behind him four coolies with a *dandy*. The note ran:

"DEAR OLD CHAP,—Come up at once. I'm monarch of all I survey. Shall expect you per return.—Yours, DICK."

Only too glad was the "super" when Forster asked permission to go; a disabled man was worse than no assistant at all. It didn't take long to gather his belongings together.

Then he was helped into the *dandy*, for he was woefully weak, and carried over hill and down dale until the four coolies pulled up at Berkeley's bungalow. Berkeley was a lucky man now. As superintendent of one of the finest tea-gardens in the Island and a Government *V.C.*, he was not lacking rupees. Furthermore he was practically his own master, and save for the occasional visit of one of the proprietors who soon wearied of the monotony of life on the hills of Ceylon, as who does not? he *was* as he said, "monarch of all he surveyed."

To "ensure something to eat," as he put it, he kept a whole family, a wise plan out there, where native servants are apt to be *non est* when most needed or laid low with "fe-var, sar," which interpreted often spells arrack, opium or *bhang*. "It's the old game of family-coach with these natives, perpetual dropping in and dropping out. The only way to ensure *one* is to tolerate a *gang*," was the advice of an old stager.

But no sooner did the *dandy* pull up, than a hearty voice greeted the occupant.

"Delighted to see you, old man. You'll soon pull round here—delightful air! And the new doctor at the hospital's a very decent chap, although a *Burgher*—he'll physic you. He comes in to take a hand at crib. There's the hospital, which, by the way, I give a wide berth. I loathe these ghastly diseases of the East. Ah! here he comes!" Coming up the bridle-path was a spare sallow man, with a swinging gait and a pair of intensely intelligent eyes—a typical *Burgher*.

"Good-day, doctor. Allow me to introduce you to my friend Forster—Dr. Maartens, Mr. Forster."

The two shook hands, and all three entered into conversation, but notwithstanding the would-be geniality, there was a certain restraint, as there always is betwixt Europeans and the descendants of the Dutch. Well, Forster made speedy recovery, thanks to change of air, good living and being well looked after.

"But no sooner on your legs than you want to be off, you're a nice chap, got another advertisement in the *Ceylon Times*, I see," said Berkeley.

Forster laughed.

"Not that I *want* to be off, you know that. But I wasn't born with the proverbial silver spoon—you know that also. I don't want to be a burden on the Mater. I know the struggle she had to get that £300 premium. I want to return it—soon as possible. But—" and a sigh escaped his lips, "I *have* had bad luck! But for *you*——"

"Pshaw! Never look back, always ahead. But not at the hospital, stuck there to obstruct a glorious view. By the way, you're going over to inspect the fever-box——"

"Yes, this afternoon. That doctor's a clever chap and I'll not forget his attention to me. Here's the post."

Berkeley took the letters. Three for himself, none for his guest. So it went on day after day. Once or twice he did get a bite in answer to his advertisement, but nothing came of it. "Just my luck," he kept on repeating. "Berkeley, dear boy, I'm getting tired of it," he said that morning.

"It isn't too lively up here," was the reply.

"No, no, I don't mean that. Tired of this bad luck—tired of life, in fact."

"*Liver!* We'll do gymnastics on our *tats*. There's a wonderful temple you've not explored But do the fever-box first. I'll not be ready till 6. Will call for you and save you the trouble of coming back. Now for the shrub, and the reckoning!" and off went Berkeley whistling.

At about four o'clock Forster made his way

to the hospital where he was received by Dr. Maartens, who took him round.

Everything was neat and trim and reflected great credit on the officer in charge. Forster was congratulating him when his attention was caught by a queer sort of object asquat but bolt upright in a corner, his long, lean, brown arms upraised over his head, his eyes fixed in a seemingly sightless gaze on his finger-tips; his body emaciated and his flowing hair burnt orange-red, tangled, dusty and matlike, the only sign of animation being in the lips which moved perpetually to a droning monotone.

"Queer lot that, doctor?" remarked Forster pointing with his riding-cane.

"A fakir—and an obstinate brute, to boot. No end of trouble these chaps cause. Not for the life of him will he submit to an operation. That man's suffering agonies, yet he goes on droning, not a morsel of food having passed his lips, nor for an instant have his eyes closed in sleep—droning—always droning."

"What's it all about?"

The doctor shrugged his shoulders. "God knows. Don't go too near. He's isolated. Even the natives give these fellows a wide berth, although they *do* half reverence them."

But Forster's interest was aroused. He knew something of hypnotism too.

"What do you bet I don't make him move his optics?" he asked.

"Half my next year's Government pay," was the answer. "Stay, for God's sake——"

But Forster was already by the *fakir's* side *suggesting* that he should turn down his "optics" and look him straight in the face. Presently the upturned gaze relaxed and lowering the great dark eyes fastened themselves on the Englishman's. All the life, the soul, the intelligence was in those eyes searching Forster through and through, or as the latter afterwards put it, "turning him inside out, by George!" The lips ceased droning. Everything was concentrated in that gaze. It seemed scarcely human in its power.

Forster in the first moments felt "queerish," but pulling himself together held his ground, and met those wonderfully penetrating orbs with the determination of an Englishman. The lean, brown arms were still uplifted, the poise of the head was the same, only the eyes had turned, and shone now with a clairvoyant light—a light that penetrated Forster's very soul. He was transfixed by that gaze. Then, at last, those parched lips spoke, "*Where the shadow of the footprint falls, there your treasure lies.*"

Weird, fearfully weird, sounded the English words spoken by that strange, uncanny creature. Forster was staggered. Nevertheless he retained sufficient composure to say, "Tell me more." But the great black eyes rolled back in their sockets and resumed the upward gaze. The droning recommenced. No power on earth, apparently, could elicit more. Forster drew a long breath.

"By the powers, doctor, did you hear?"

Yes, Doctor Maartens had heard, and thought it expedient to move away. Like all natives of the East, he was superstitious and timid.

"*My* treasure, by Jove! What would Berkeley say to that? Ah! speak of— Just thinking of you, old man. I've had an experience. Come in."

"Not I. You know my aversion; come out. What's your experience? You can relate it as we amble along," said Berkeley.

And Foster did. But all the encouragement he got was:

"Now, don't be a fool, old chap, and don't for heaven's sake go near these beastly, filthy fakirs. You've been out in the East long enough to know what *they* are!"

All the same, Forster was haunted by that voice, those words:

"*Where the shadow of the footprint falls, there your treasure lies.*"

II

Although Forster was convalescent and desirous of being up and doing, ill-luck pursued him : he had got into a groove of it. He had been the guest of his friend Berkeley six weeks, and though Dick was just as keen on his staying "until something turned up," Forster's spirit winced under the fact of his inability to offer any sort of return. His genial companionship was on the decline too, naturally, with this load of anxiety.

"One for you, old man, and good luck to you," said his host, sorting the letters at 6 A.M. over their *chota hazira*. Forster's hand was outstretched eagerly, and his eye devoured the contents of the note in an instant :

"*Call at my office, Nuraliya, between* 10 *a.m. and* 4 *p.m. Tuesday—expenses paid.—Joskins junr.*"

"Joskins junior! That's the crank!" exclaimed Berkeley. "*Nobody* can square him. One of the wealthiest planters in Ceylon, but—*impossible!* You won't waste your time over *him* will you?"

Forster sighed. "When a man's driven to desperation——"

"Tut, tut! There's always the coach to fall back upon," put in Dick, half jokingly and referring to the "stony-broke" gentlemen who adopt up-country coach-driving as a livelihood out in Ceylon.

Forster was thinking of his "*mater*," of her hopes, her ambition, her faith in her only boy. If necessary he would encounter a jungle full of tigers—if there *were* tigers in Ceylon. Yes, by George, he'd go. Accordingly, Tuesday, 3.30 P.M., found him at the office in Nuraliya, and at 3.35 P.M., the door opening, revealed the substantial vision of a huge man, red as a tomato, with ginger whiskers, carroty hair, and small blue eyes that pierced like gimlets.

"So you want a berth like the rest of 'em?" was his greeting. Forster inclined his head. "Can't you sit down, man? Stiff in the joints? Then you won't do for me. Oh, you can, can you? Well?"

Forster coughed.

"*Well?* Can't you speak? That's your infirmity, is it? Don't want any dumb cattle here. Not without its advantage at times—plenty of chattering apes about. But—damn it, man, who's to report? Oh, you'll write, you think? No, you won't. That won't do for me. Bits of boys coming and making their conditions to me. I'll have a *verbal* report or none. *None*, I say. Do you hear, or are you deaf as well? By the Lord, was ever man so plagued! Deaf, dumb, incapable —*Punkah!* D——n that boy, he's asleep again." The speaker was well nigh exhausted after this voluble display of rhetoric, during which he had grown redder and redder, and the little steel-blue eyes fiercer and fiercer. This was the first opportunity of getting a word in in reply. Forster seized it.

"No, I'm neither deaf nor dumb, nor am I stiff in the joints. I'm all round sound and *square*—when people are *square* with me. If that's all you've got to say to me I'll wish you 'Good day.'"

"By—*Jupiter!* young 'un, there's grit in you. No whining or skulking. What have you been doing out here in this—— Testimonials? Pshaw! Rubbish! What's it to me—Joskins junior—what any fool has to say about you? Come to *Guniawalla* on the 12th; salary R500 a month—R600 if you give satisfaction. *A month*, mind, plain English—none of your *per mensem*, as one young prig I kicked out called it. Now go, and good day to you."

Forster met the outstretched hand, and in it was a bundle of paper notes left in his own, whose sum total, by the way, doubled the amount of his expenses.

He returned in high spirits, and reported his success to Berkeley, who "humphed."

Now when the 12th arrived, Forster found himself at Hatton railway station. The porters smiled when he said, "*Guniawalla Estate.*" They knew *J. J.*, as he was called. The *gharrywallah* supplemented his smile with a request that he might "bring the *Mahatmaya* back next week"—*he* knew *J. J.* also. It was a long drive, but very refreshing after the hot, dusty railway journey. Adam's Peak loomed like a presiding genius, and cast huge shadows athwart the lovely landscape as yet undestroyed by the little tea-shrub. But when at length the *gharry* pulled up at a bridle-path there was neither *tat* nor rickshaw, so Forster had to put the best foot first and mount.

"Good luck, sar," with a very broad grin from the gharry driver, pocketing his fare and an extra *santosum.*

Forster was equal to the mount. He enjoyed it; the fresh air was new life to him, as it always is in Ceylon. The entire hill was carpeted with sunlight—the *setting* sun, whose heat being modified made it pleasant and exhilarating. The zig-zag path opened out fresh vistas of beautiful landscape, although the hill itself was thickly planted with the tea-shrub, which is *not* a thing of beauty.

Farther up, a turn brought him to an open space, cleared presumably for planting. Over this space lay shade. A shadow seemed to rest upon it. Forster relieved himself of his smoked glasses—they were not required. Sunlit still was all the land around, but here was shade, a shadow —cast by what?

He turned his regards around to answer. There was Adam's Peak still with the sunlight full upon the mountain, which only brought out that strange mark called by the Sinhalese *Buddha's Footprint* in stronger contrast, while here on the ground where he stood was shadow. The closer he observed the more assured was he that that shadow took the form of the "Foot-print." Simultaneously the words of the *fakir* flashed into his mind:

"*Where the shadow of the Footprint falls, there your treasure lies.*"

III

Letter addressed to R. BERKELEY, ESQ.

GUNIAWALLA, *June 11th.*

DEAR OLD CHAP,—Been here just a week. Can't stand much more of it. Said I'd go this morning; answer, a growl. Bad luck! Bad luck! Can you put me up on my way to Colombo? —Yours, HARRY FORSTER.

P.S.—Something curious about this place. Will relate when we meet.

Photo. Platé, Ceylon

A WATER-FALL ON THE HILLS OF CEYLON WITH ADAM'S PEAK IN THE DISTANCE. THE FOOTPRINT CAN BE SEEN UPON THE SIDE OF THE MOUNTAIN

"Poor devil!" was Berkeley's comment. Then he wrote a telegram: "Come at once."

Now it happened, chanced some might say—but I don't believe in chance—well, it happened that betwixt the writing of the above note and receipt of the "wire" something occurred. All through the heat of the day Forster had been attending to his duties, with a heart of lead, as many of us have often to do.

"Nothing for it but to throw myself on good old Dick!" he kept on repeating to himself. "I'm an unlucky dog; but—there's always the coach. Better fellows than I have to come to it, and—the *mater* needn't know." Then he leaned back in his chair in the tea factory. So delightful the shade after hours under the blazing sun! So heavenly, beyond the eye and hearing of *J. J.!* "Last time I shall 'tiff' with him," he was thinking, "Why are such monsters born? Why are such iniquities allowed to live, and thrive, and prosper? My God! this life's a riddle?" With this he laid his head on the desk thinking, thinking what he should, what on earth he *could* do. But his thoughts were interrupted by a strange noise.

"Hullo! a cheetah in trouble in the jungle. What a weird, plaintive cry! Quite a human ring in it. A female mourning its cub, evidently. If so the chance of sport's lost—pity!" He had risen and was following the direction of the weird cry. It brought him to a well in that part where the shadow always rested. It was there now.

"By Jove, it's *in* the well. Hi! hullo there!" he shouted, making all the noise he could. A cry, half moan, half groan came from the bottom of the well. The water was shallow, but the well was deep, very deep. Looking down Forster could distinguish a huge white substance that moved.

Weeds and maidenhair fern grew in profusion on the side of the well and amongst them he fancied he saw a *solar topee* such as was worn by *J. J.*

"My God!" ejaculated Forster. "*J. J.!*" and a thought seized him, "should he let him remain?" A few minutes, a few seconds perhaps, and the world would be rid of ——

Nobody would be the wiser. It was an unused well. Nobody came there. On that land where the shadow fell nothing would grow. It was hallowed or accursed, the coolies said. *Nobody would ever know.* These thoughts coursed his mind like lightning, gripped him for the nonce. Next moment the whistle was at his lips—the whistle he used to summon the coolies. He blew lustily. Once, twice, *thrice*—the danger signal, which meant a *santosum* at the end of it. A dozen coolies appeared instanter.

"Fetch a rope, a chain from the factory. The first back shall have R20," cried Forster, bending over the well.

Both chain and rope were fetched in a twinkling and lowered down the well.

"Fasten round the body. We'll have you out, never fear," shouted Forster. Then to the coolies, "Hold on, hoist, for all you're worth." A dozen brown hands seized the rope and chain. Nevertheless, Forster had to bear the brunt; the Sinhalese is a poor specimen of mankind. Presently the bulky form of Joskins Junior arose above the water, and as it continued to rise, one leg had the appearance of being broken. "Poor old chap!" murmured Forster, the sweat pouring down his brow, his fair hair darkening and matting with it, his shirt wringing wet.

"Hold on, for God's sake!" he shouted, for the effort was such that he felt his strength might not meet it. *If it should give way!* God! a human life was at stake. This thought braced him. The weight of a body normally eighteen stone was that of a rhinoceros now. With the reward in view the coolies kept their hold. The fact of their daily sustenance depending on it, would not have sufficed. The coolie is like a child, a sugar plum given now is more to be valued than any future store. Therefore, they held on—for the ten rupees: held on and hoisted with all the strength and muscle nature had given them, the Englishman's equalling the whole half dozen. But there was a limit to his. He was just conscious of this fact when another good haul brought the burden to the top and deposited it on *terra firma*, inert and insensible. A *dandy* was fetched, and the unconscious body of Joskins Junior laid thereon, and carried up to the bungalow. While a coolie was despatched for the nearest doctor, Forster set about restoring animation. The doctor being in came at once and set the fractured limb.

"A timely and heroic action, Mr. Forster, say what you will. Yes, he is conscious now, and going on all right. That immersion in the cold water was his salvation. A sudden attack of heat apoplexy, which with his temperament and constitution might have proved serious. You came in the nick of time, for had he lost consciousness, he might have been drowned even in that shallow depth of water. He is indebted for his life to you. But—you'll not think of leaving him now, as I hear you purpose doing to-morrow?"

Forster pulled a long face, "My friend expects me"——

A slight twinkle came into the doctor's eye. "I know; but if you could manage another week, say. It's an action of humanity. Put it to yourself in that way, Mr. Forster."

Forster heaved a sigh; the doctor smiled sympathetically.

"I'll try to send some one up to look after him—I'll *try*. But, meanwhile," with entreaty in the tone,

"Right you are." Forster braced himself to reply. "I'll stay, and—wire Berkeley."

"Thanks, thanks," and the doctor shook Forster cordially by the hand. "I'll come up to-morrow. A fine estate this. How distinct the Footprint is to-day. Quite a phenomenon isn't it? that shadow? There's a superstition about it amongst the local natives. The shrubs would never thrive on that spot"—

"They will now. I don't see why they didn't before," interrupted Forster.

"May be you have broken the spell. They say some white man was to do it. Well, you deserve good luck. Let's hope you'll have it. Good-bye."

The following telegram was then sent off to Berkeley:

"Fates dispose. Can't leave yet. Will write.

"FORSTER."

If ever Forster had a difficult time as well as a disagreeable one, it was now when he acted nurse to Joskins Junior; even the native coolies commiserated him. All would have deserted, but for him, and the promised *santosum*.

A little forest of arms was outstretched into the window of the sick chamber soon after the doctor left.

"What do they want, the rascals, their pay? They've had it," growled the invalid, attempting to lay hold of his stick and provoking pain in the newly set limb which evoked a savage howl.

"Pray be careful. Anything you want I will do," said Forster.

"Then, fling this stick at their heads—the villains!"

"All right: don't distress yourself. I'll send them away."

More easily said than done.

"Be off, you rascals. You'd rob a dying man," chimed in *J. J.*, his face growing purple with passion. But again, the hands and arms appeared through the window, and voices clamoured for the *santosum* which Forster hadn't in his possession to give. He went to the door, and explained—"to-morrow, perhaps." But "to-morrow" would not do. They wanted it *now*, and were obdurate, utterly unheedful too of the master's shouts and threats, knowing he couldn't get after them. Ultimately they turned away sullenly. Not another stroke of work would they do until the promised *santosum* was forthcoming. This the vow uppermost in each mind, and this vow they kept, one and all. The rest of the coolies following suit, all banded together on strike, men, women and children. And just when labour and attention were most needed!

"What are those rascals doing?" was *J. J.'s* persistent inquiry, so that Forster was obliged to tell him, as gently as possible, out of consideration for his condition. Nevertheless, had he spoken in a voice of thunder, punctuated with thunderbolts, the result could not have been worse.

"What! *What!* Twenty rupees each! They shan't have it, the villains!"

Fortunately the doctor entering put a stop to more ebullition by administering a quieting dose, while Forster effected a temporary conciliation by giving each coolie five rupees out of his own pocket, the consequence being—coolies *non est* for a couple of days and the tavern profiting. No one could the doctor find to take Forster's place. Forster was compelled to stay on. Night and day he had to be in attendance, and when at the end of the second week he said he really must be off, the suggestion produced a relapse.

"He wants to kill me, doctor, leaving me to die like a hound! Hurrh!" and the sick man groaned for pity—or with rage.

"It's hard on you, I know, Mr. Forster, but—humanity. Who is there to take your place? *Nobody!*" The doctor might have said, "Who *would?*" So another wire was sent to Berkeley, who, although heartily commiserating his friend, replied, "You are right to remain a while longer, but rely on a welcome when you *can* come.—Yours, DICK."

One day, from out a volley of moans and groans Joskins Junior spoke:

"Forster, are you there? Humph! Not deserted me yet, though you mean to, hey? I want you to write a note:

"'Messrs. Sharp and Clipper, Colombo: Come at once.—JOSKINS JUNIOR.'

"No! not a wire. Didn't I say a *note?*

"'Come at once.—JOSKINS JUNIOR.'"

Forster did as he was requested.

"Short and to the point. That will do. Now give it to that black devil and draw the blinds, and let more light come in. What are those rascals doing? Hurrh! To-morrow—to-morrow, I'll be after them! I—want to sleep now." Saying which he turned over and was soon asleep.

For the first time for three weeks Forster got a couple of hours' release. Most of that night and of next day the invalid slept, and Forster was free to wander and inspect and enjoy the air. The shadows were lengthening when, as he hurried back to the bungalow one day he overtook two gentlemen, one of whom he recognised immediately as the doctor, the other was Mr. Clipper, of the legal firm of Sharp and Clipper, Colombo. The three walked up together ; then, Forster preceding, they entered the sick room. The patient was wide awake and seemed wonderfully composed. Only a little of his "temperament" showed itself on the doctor's asking him how he felt.

"*Feel?* Never better in my life. Stay, I want you, though—both of you. *You* (to Forster) may go."

Forster accordingly strolled out on to the verandah. The setting sun cast long weird shadows, and when he turned he found himself in full view of the Shadow of the Footprint—Buddha's Footprint—on Adam's Peak, blacker, more distinct than ever this evening.

"Whew! It'll take a heavier foot than that to stamp out my work," he said, for the little nursery of tea-shrubs was thriving now. Then suddenly his thoughts reverted to the *fakir* in the hospital that day and the words said to him :

"*Where the shadow of the Footprint falls there your treasure lies!*"

Forster laughed.

"The fellow wasn't far out—only in the personality. That crop will help to fill the coffers of *J. J.*—thanks to me! I bring luck to *others*, it seems." Then he sighed. "Where shall I be this time next week? With Dick, dear old chap; a true friend—in need."

"Mr. Forster, will you come, please? Mr. Joskins asks for you."

It was Mr. Clipper who spoke. Forster obeyed, and entering, was beckoned by the doctor to the bed. At a glance the truth was revealed to him —*Joskins Junior was dying.*

"My God!" he ejaculated under his breath, for the suddenness was a shock to him, and withal a painful shock, for had he not been the dying man's constant attendant night and day? Ay, and there is a tie throughout humanity, that "one touch of nature" that stirs our fine emotions when the parting comes, no matter what the conditions may have been.

Joskins Junior raised his eyes, tried to raise his hand, his voice, but failed, looked Forster full in the face, then closed his eyes and died.

"Heart failure. Nothing on earth could save him," said the doctor. "I knew it as soon as I saw him this evening."

. . . .

Copy of the last Will and Testament of Josiah Joskins Junior, of *Guniawalla* Estate, Ceylon.

I, Josiah Joskins, of Guniawalla Estate, and of Nuraliya, Ceylon, give and bequeath the said estate and the whole of my property and personal belongings to Henry Forster, who has not told me one lie since he came to me three months ago.

(Signed) JOSIAH JOSKINS.

In presence of Wilfred Maartens, M.D., and Richard Clipper, solicitor.

Forster's luck came at last—"where the Shadow of the Footprint fell."

CHAPTER IX

Gipsying in the moonlight — A perfect dreamland: with curious inhabitants, though!—They fall in with a fakir —Two prophecies: one fulfilled — A rogue-elephant abroad — Government reward of £5 offered — Cynthia's resolve —A midnight call on Mohammedans — A *minah* present and a *houri* compliment.

THERE was little sleep that night at the rest-house (*Ambalama*), seeing that it was a case of move on at daybreak in order to avoid the heat. Consequently by noon, after an excellent tiffin cooked under a huge mahogany tree, all were inclined for a *siesta.*

Although the floor of the cart was not downy —no amount of rugs could make it that—the travellers enjoyed some hours of refreshing sleep. A cup of tea on awaking made them fit to continue the journey at sunset.

Of a truth this night travelling was enjoyable! It made them renounce day journeying altogether, for besides the heat was the glare. Insects there were at all times, albeit Cynthia showered Keating's powder with reckless extravagance, seeing that it costs 50 cents a small tin out there. The villagers would pause in their paddy-grinding to stare, particularly at the white *Nona* with "clothes" on her hands.

But in a day or two the travellers got beyond the villages, and the few pedestrians they met were of a very low type, their brains too stagnant even for curiosity. One queer specimen was deserving of remark. Cynthia labelled it "a peregrinatory bundle of bones, leather-bound," and insisted upon stopping to "interview." *It* was a *fakir*.

The services of the Indian cook were requisitioned, he being the only one of the party conversant with *Hindi*, or *Hindoostani*, as it is wrongly called.

In this wise they learnt this "bundle of bones, leather-bound," this *fakir*, to be more polite—had pilgrimaged the length and breadth of India, likewise of Burmah and Thibet.

Years of ascetic life and rigorous training had developed occult powers which he generously declared all possess.

Would the *Sahib* like to witness some manifestation of these powers? He would. Very good.

The *fakir* forthwith commenced to unpack the burden on his back, the principal item being a bamboo framework or scaffolding. This he held with his right hand, while he mounted step by step of bamboos. At the summit—a height perhaps of eleven feet—he paused, with arms extended, to effect a balance. For some reason or other the framework remained perfectly steady and perpendicular, while the *fakir* stretched himself out like a spider on its web. At intervals on the bamboos were huge nails, rusty, but sharp at the point. These nails distinctly penetrated the man's mahogany-coloured flesh when he stretched himself out on the framework. Thus he remained, a hideous wound made by each nail, from which the purple blood flowed—remained thus for the space of ten minutes or so; excepting for the blood, a lifeless figure of clay. Then, muttering some strange gibberish, animation returned, and making movements so that the nails were extricated from the wounds, the *fakir* with his toes kicked away the scaffolding and remained himself alone *unsupported in mid-air*. Yes, there this weird creature remained, his lean, chocolate-coloured limbs apparently stiff and cataleptic, his eyes fixed upwards and glazed.

"It's a fact," said Cynthia in low tones of wonder. "At home they would say we were hypnotised."

Presently the limbs became more life-like, mobile. The *fakir* drew a long, deep breath, then sprang to the ground. Other feats this queer being accomplished, but all savoured of the same —mortification of the flesh and disregard of recognised laws of nature. They had an uncanny flavour, and conveyed an indescribably disagreeable impression, or rather sensation.

"Abnormal creature!" ejaculated Cynthia; "he's a nightmare! Can he see into the future?"

Whereupon the cook put the question, translating this reply, given while the *fakir* stared into Cynthia's eyes with orbs like two coppery-red suns:

"This lady has travelled much and will travel much more. Her friends are of high caste: they understand her best. She has many enemies. Her best deeds are fated to make her worst enemies. She will live to old age and die in plenty. A life of adventures, but more of sadness than of joy."

Then turning to Cynthia's husband:

"Sir, your troubles will be all over in three years." (Just within the time specified Cynthia was left a widow.) A few rupees, a bag of rice, and this gruesome *fakir* went on his way. Then pandemonium, when creatures of the jungle before retiring to rest assemble and hold parliament. Parrots and parakeets, coming in flocks and screaming on the wing; monkeys, chattering and quarrelling; cheetahs, jackals, boars, buffaloes, elephants, roaring, howling, trumpeting; the king of the jungle—the elephant's voice above them all. Now, before leaving Colombo, they had read in the newspapers of a reward offered by Government for the capture, dead or alive, of a "rogue elephant," which was committing no end of mischief and wanton destruction in the village—a peril to villagers and to property.

"What if we gained the reward!" said Cynthia, eyeing the gun, always loaded ready for use. "The vulnerable part, the back of the ear; don't forget, should we encounter the big "black sheep." Worst of it is *my* heart always softens to naughtiness—it's so nice! Hark! that must be he!"

The whole earth seemed to vibrate; but this was the *finale*. Thunder-like reverberations died away in the distant jungle, then all was quiet. Peace, perfect peace. And oh! the loveliness, the glory of the night! All Nature was at rest. But no! As they walked—for walking was preferable, far, to jogging and jolting in the cart these cool, moonlight nights—as they walked they constantly kicked itinerant somethings of various sizes—tortoises, from the size of a penny-piece to that of a dinner-plate, out for a constitutional. During the heat of the day they rest in the bed of streams. The tiny young ones are really beautiful: their shells are so transparent and delicate. Cynthia wanted a nursery of them. But, alas! young things grow old alike throughout Nature, and when reminded of this sad fact she recollected a tortoise-pet of her nursery days. Dear, hideous old thing! how patiently he had drawn the cart-load of white mice in their game of "gipsying"! That was a game, this reality. And yet it scarcely seemed so. The moonlight and the landscape were so romantic, so ideal. The day brought so many worries—the monkeys worst of all. Just as they were about to fall into a delightful slumber a long hairy arm would be thrust in, and seizing Cynthia's plaited hair tug away at it vigorously, or a fight would take place on the *cadjan* roof for possession of something looted by one bolder than the rest. In this way Cynthia's "green goggles" went, and she had the satisfaction of seeing them adorn the nasal organ of a hideous monster high up in a mahogany-tree. They were a perfect pest, these monkeys—re-incarnations of all the sinful attributes and actions of imperfect humanity, the Theosophists might say.

But after another day, or rather night's, travelling they observed traces of cultivation, and presently a trim little bungalow, with blue-painted lintels and window sills, came into view. Mahommedans, of course; for are not the followers of Islam the cleanest and most decent-living people in the East? Pity 'tis, 'tis true.

"Let's make as much noise as possible and wake them up. I'm in just the mood for a moonlight call," said Cynthia, commencing to sing and kick about the tortoises. It had the desired effect, for what looked like a bundle on the verandah moved; another bundle moved. Bundle No. 1 had a voice, for it spoke; bundle No. 2 ditto, for it answered. Both bundles rose and came forward.

"Good evening," said Cynthia in her most winsome tones.

"*Salaam Mahatmaya: Nona Salaam.*"

Both, *still* bundles (Cynthia was glad of that), greeted and bowed low.

"May we—er—call upon you? Never mind the bungalow, the verandah will do," continued Cynthia, making for a Singapore chair.

"*Nona Salaam!*" came another greeting close behind. Cynthia looked, but saw no one. Meanwhile the Mohammedans were offering cocoanut water, whisky and soda, tonic water, and oranges, and at the same time satisfying their curiosity as to the identity of their visitors. They had heard that a gentleman in the Government Service had bought land in that district for planting. It was good soil—they had proved it—and must prove profitable.

"*Nona Salaam.*" Again Cynthia turned, but could see no one. "Some one behind the purdah," thought she. "Er—may, *might* I see your—ladies?" she asked in her sweetest of voices.

The two men looked at one another, and an awkward silence ensued. "Your wives, I mean," added Cynthia, which, instead of mending, appeared to make matters worse.

"*Nona Salaam,*" again from behind.

"I thought, as they were so kind in greeting me, they must be awake, and—might like to see me."

"Ah, the *minah!*" exclaimed one of the men, proceding to take down a cage in which was one of these birds, quite wide awake and very much inclined to be communicative.

"Then it was this who greeted? Really! What a wonderful bird! Does it speak English?" As if in answer the bird promptly replied:

"Hard up, lady—Unlucky devil—Poor chap!" as distinctly as she could say it herself.

Yes, indeed, *minahs are* wonderful birds. Their attachment is so great, moreover, that to them literally there is "no place like home." They must, therefore, be domiciled when mere fledglings, otherwise they would find their way home be it ever so far away.

On parting, a young *minah* in a trim little cage was handed as a present to Cynthia, which evoked this response.

"I think you Mohammedans charming people, although you wouldn't admit me, being a woman, to your heaven!" To which the younger and handsomer made reply:

"Oh, but we *have houris?*" Not so bad for a heathen—was it?

CHAPTER X

Puggarees to be pinned up—Mischievous monkeys —Cook, the consoler — A webby-white ghost visible in the moonlight—A prize for the Psychical Research Society—Human supremacy: and conceit—Life not worth a moment's purchase in the Paradise of Adam.

ABOUT sunset, jackals and porcupines, peacocks, wild cats and cheetahs would emerge from the jungle and take a look at the caravan, but they appeared more frightened far than the human occupants. The monkeys continued their mischievous tricks, making determined efforts to relieve the travellers of their *puggarees*, which were too safely secured, however. It isn't pleasant all the same to have one's head nearly pulled off, so the *puggarees* had to be pinned up. Whatever they succeeded in purloining they fought for, and the battle royal often as not took place on the roof of the cart, to its detriment sometimes, inasmuch as a brown limb would protrude; afterwards the shrieking in getting it extricated was ear-splitting. Though the country now abounded with animal-life, not a human being was to be seen. Adam's Peak loomed as ever a landmark and a guide. Frequently that peculiar "hiss" heralded the approach of the cobra, who, with head erect, would gaze at the travellers as though asking, "Who are you? What business have you here?" Tic-polongas in plenty there were too. It seemed incredible that this was the same world as our London with its streets and its shops, and its throng of hustling humanity. And yet, not as now was it here ages ago. Then this part of *Lanka* was thickly populated by the aboriginal *Vedda*, not many of whom remain, although had they penetrated the jungle they might have encountered a few. They have not the audacity of monkeys, these *Veddo*; shyness is a product of evolution only developed in the human.

There is a bird in Ceylon the natives call "the devil," as they believe it to be the precursor of evil, bad luck, or death. It is a huge owl, and has a weird and mournful cry.

"That bird always come after this 'caravan,'" said the cook consolingly. It was a fact though. It haunted them, "like an evil genius," Cynthia said. One night as they were jogging along, near midnight, they beheld a ghost. What else could that shadowy, opal-white form be that moved, actually moved, in the moonlight? It had been one of the many dreams of Cynthia's girlhood to find herself face to face with a ghost, not a "faked up" modern "materialisation," but a genuine old-fashioned webby-white transparent ghost. Here surely it was!

"Gracious heavens! A ghost!" she exclaimed as the diaphanous mass evolved itself before their very eyes. Would it come nearer? Even the little bulls could see it; no clairvoyance was this. A veritable ghost in the act of shaping itself for its midnight walks abroad. The bulls stopped and jibbed at it. Nothing would induce them to go on while *It* evolved. It required no eye-strain to behold a huge mass forming, a mass whiter than the moonlight, and ghastlier. All were sound asleep in the cart but themselves on foot, and the bulls who refused to move, apparently stricken with terror. What should they do? Waken the cook?

Now this was easier said than done, as all are aware who know the native. However, it *was* accomplished. Rubbing his sleepy eyes and looking ahead he saw It—the ghost. Cynthia was prepared for a howl and a hasty retreat.

But, nothing of the kind.

"Devil's Trumpet," said he complacently. "Big Devil that, have such big trumpet. See, Lady, opening now. Only at night in moonlight that flower open. Devil blow plenty nice smell through that trumpet. Lady smell it?" Cynthia did, for now a sweet but too powerful perfume filled the air. So it was a flower this ghostly object, a midnight blossom, which when fully open takes the form of a monster trumpet, called by the natives in consequence—for everything huge and mighty is accredited to the *diavolo*—the Devil's Trumpet. Its fragrance is not only languorously sweet but contains narcotic properties which speedily produce drowsiness. Cynthia was just beginning to experience this effect when she received a severe blow on the head which at another time might have stunned.

Now it aroused her. It was a gargantuan centipede, resembling a bar of gold some eleven inches in length, with a hundred slender branches by way of limbs and emerald green eyes. A beautiful work of art rather than of nature, it looked. What a necklet for some slender white throat! Cynthia was thinking as it lay there in the road. But when its lobster-like claws opene and closed, and the fine feathery sting went awagging, she envied not the society beauty who would wear it! Her own escape had been narrow enough.

Now the consciousness of human supremacy is very gratifying, though it *may* be based on human conceit. As a matter of fact, human life in some quarters of God's earth is not worth a moment's purchase. A sting from one of the least of these inferior creatures—that tiny green fly or yonder tarantula may take both conceit and breath out of a giant in less time than it takes to tell.

Nevertheless, Man is Lord of Creation, and is never more proudly conscious of the fact than when encompassed by creatures that could quench his spark of life in a few minutes, as in the Paradise of Adam.

CHAPTER XI

A scene from Macbeth — How Cynthia took her matutinal tub — Devastation; desolation — Driving a pair of miniature bulls *not* in the native way—They pay a visit to an ancient rock temple —A Buddhist monk and the modern madam over the top of a palm-leaf fan — "Such treasure! Such waste!"—An "awful example!"—Was this the "rogue"?

IT was only the mud verandah where they sat and supped some three nights later, but the moon shone radiantly upon them, and with gun and revolvers in readiness, a mongoose, and fires burning briskly all around to keep away snakes, and wholesome viands cooked to a turn—what could human beings want more?

The voices of the little encampment sounded strangely in the midnight jungle. The natives moving about looked like figures in a shadow pantomime, while Cynthia's appearance might have suggested one of Macbeth's witches and her husband's Mephisto. It was well on in the morn when they sought their couches. Nevertheless the sun had just risen when they took their bath.

Distinctly primitive is it to stand in a stream

pouring water from a *calabash* over one's head. This is the native and most healthy way of bathing, however. If Europeans would but adopt it, we should not hear so much of that "touch of the liver" so general in the tropics. After this and a cup of tea and "string *appas*" they felt "fit." The daylight though revealed one disagreeable fact—the estate had been allowed to go to rack and ruin! Notwithstanding the fact of the monthly remittances to cover salary of the superintendent, coolies' pay, renovations in the way of fencing after attacks of invading boars and buffaloes, "nursery" planting, &c. &c., nothing had been done apparently for months. Jungle, nought but jungle, the few plants there were being choked by it. Where was the superintendent? No one knew. The two coolies were dispatched to bring a full force of male agricultural labourers, and would not be likely to return before evening. What to do meanwhile? There was the cart, but who was to drive?

"Come along. We'll drive—somehow," said Cynthia." "The bulls are in the stream. Cook will get them out."

Cook did, and furthermore volunteered to assist in harnessing, that is, getting the rope through the beasts' noses. Hindoos are far more obliging than Sinhalese. With a store of light provisions and corresponding hearts off they set. The climate here was much cooler than Colombo, the air was fresh and invigorating. The scenery, at intervals between the jungle, appeared to Cynthia to be made up of bits from every country in Europe, only that in Ceylon the trees are of huger proportions and never leafless. One peculiarity of this island is that the cobra or its outline permeates all nature. One sees it twining round the plantains, on the bark of trees, as a parasite climbing the trunk, on stones, rocks, everywhere.

Our travellers little knew what they were undertaking in attempting to drive a pair of miniature bulls. Presumably they—the bulls—missed the customary means of goading, biting their tails and probing the awful sores on their haunches ; *go* they would not, or if they did it was at their own sweet will.

It was well on in the afternoon when they pulled up at the Rock Temple for inspection.

In the towering cliff of massive rock was a footway of uneven steps, evidently the work of man ages upon ages ago, judging from the worn condition. The afternoon sun beat fiercely on the rock, giving back terrific heat. It *was* a mount.

But the view alone was worth it—so Cynthia thought. The broad, blue Indian Ocean, in which the Maldive Islands looked like green-backed turtles : the whole extent of Ceylon, that pearl pendant from India's wonderful land, with Adam's

Peak and Adam's Footprint * always and for ever in view.

The sole sign of vegetation at top of the rock was the *Ficus Religiosa*, or Sacred Bo-Tree. There it stood, centuries old, sheltering the shrine, erstwhile Hindú, Buddhist now. Perhaps one might more correctly say both—Hindú-Buddhist—for within, the *Vihara* is a queer pantheon of gods, goddesses and demons, in the midst of which Siddharta in the three postures gazes with sorrow-laden eyes. The panelling of alternate ivory and silver is encrusted with the grime and cobwebs of centuries.

"Such treasure! Such waste!" sighed Cynthia. The monk, their guide, however, could not understand such lamentation any more than he could the cut of her tailor-made coat and skirt, which, by the way, he eyed not disapprovingly from over the top of his palm leaf, always provided against the alluring glance of woman. The altars, laden with the waxen blossoms of orange, areca, and myrtle, helped to make the heavy air still more stifling, while insects were there in billions. One huge furry spider spread half across the face of a monster wooden Buddha. In a community of gem-studded gods in gold, silver, and ivory was a black one, carved in ebony. This was *Krishna*, and

* Christians say Adam's, Buddhists say Buddha's Footprint.

surrounding him were the milkmaids, semi-draped, bold-looking young women.

Cynthia heaved a sigh of relief on returning to fresh air.

"Well," said she, "if there be anything in 'storing up merit' I reckon I've secured a fair amount this morning, for never before did I encounter my two 'holiest horrors,' dirt and spiders, as in that temple!"

The return journey was a problem in gymnastics for all concerned. The only explanation being that one of the demons, or a company, had come out for a holiday and obsessed the little bulls.

Upon arrival, Cynthia immediately sought rest, uttering but one word—"Tea."

As answer there came an awful thud on the roof above, speedily followed by a cloud of dust, with glimpse of the sky beyond, and much squeaking and squealing, fluttering and flapping. Again a thud, and down came a heavy weight upon Cynthia's limbs. Not by nature given to screaming, Cynthia did now—with all the power of her lungs. A huge black object with wings in a frantic state of flutter, the size and weight of an infant, lay in her lap. The light was too dim to discern what it was.

Cynthia, meanwhile struggling to escape, cried, Send for the cook, and a light!"

Both forthcoming, the former proceeded to inspect with his kitchen lamp—the usual lighted wick afloat in an eau-de-Cologne bottle. A smile illumined his dark features when he said:

"Flying fox, sar."

By this time the uninvited visitor was quiet, in fact, abnormally still.

"Poor thing, it has fainted!" said Cynthia recovering herself and turning on a spray of *eau-de-Cologne* from another bottle—always at hand.

The Cook's broad smile broadened still more.

"No faint, Lady. Flying fox been at toddy. Toddy drawing season. Too much drunk."

"*What!*" Cynthia, inclined almost to fanatic principles *re* the "drink question," shrieked.

"Lady hear monkeys in jungle make much noise in toddy-drawing season; all get much drunk, then quarrel, fight. No constable come take 'way monkey. Very bad time this, lady."

Incredible as this may seem, it was a fact. This, then, accounted for much of the pandemonium going on until the small hours of the morning—*Toddy!* *

That night in the moonlight the coolies returned with some forty odd others. Poor emaciated creatures, there appeared little stamina in them for the hard work of clearing the jungle. But,

* This Toddy is like a mixture of champagne and ginger beer, and is very intoxicating.

like our British workman, they know how to take work in homœopathic doses. It was useless to attempt to sleep until the inhabitants of the jungle quieted down. And this was not before the hour preceding dawn. Cynthia was then composing herself for sleep, when another disturbance occurred: a rustling against the mud wall inside the bungalow, the camp beds being as usual in the centre. Carefully raising the mosquito-net with one hand, the other on a loaded revolver, Cynthia peered out. A small lamp burning sufficed to reveal a strange object—a long dark proboscis swinging pendulum-fashion, behind which, and in the framework of the open window, two very bright though small eyes shone like glittering diamonds.

"An elephant! Can it be the 'Rogue'?" was Cynthia's immediate thought. No, she would not shoot. What if she missed aim? Death, certain death. Besides, had she not recollections of youth and "Zoo days," and Jumbo, dear Jumbo!

A tin of Huntley and Palmer's biscuits was within reach. She threw one. It was caught in the trunk, conveyed to the mouth, and the trunk stretched out for more. Another was thrown, and another, until none were left. There were the morning's *appas*, but these were beyond reach. How could she get them without getting up? Cynthia's courage didn't extend to that.

Meanwhile the trunk was stretched far as it would go, and a little, very little, voice said, "Wee! wee!"

Get those *appas* she must. Perhaps their lives depended on it. At this moment her husband awoke.

"What are you doing, sitting up like that? My God! what's that?"

"Hush! be quiet! Give me those *appas*. It's all right."

"Right! It's the Rogue. The gun——"

"No," said Cynthia. "No. I entreat you not. Give me those *appas*. Now, see!" And one after another was thrown, caught, and eaten by the visitor, until all were gone.

Then, gracefully swinging his trunk a moment or two he drew it out and took his departure.

Was this indeed the Rogue? At the thought Cynthia now went—well, limp.

CHAPTER XII

Cynthia's first "at home" in the jungle—A shock to woman's vanity—A good night's rest disturbed—An alarm — Wild buffaloes break in—All up and armed—Exciting spectacle in the moonlight—Bungalow and occupants in deadly danger — A majestic presence—"An elephant, by Jove!"—"Dear old rogue!"

AT 6 A.M. the firing of the gun was the signal for the coolies to assemble. They obeyed, with laggard step and sullen countenance. Not an interesting group by any stretch of the imagination. Where was the superintendent? Still *non est*. Nobody knew; nobody ever does in Ceylon. The coolies commenced hacking away with the mamoties. Not so very difficult to get thus far, but to keep them at it! As soon as the *white* backs turned, down went the mamoties. Without supervision nothing would have been done. The narcotic and poisonous fumes emitted by the undergrowth caused such vertigo Cynthia was compelled to return to the bungalow and while away the dreary day with the aid of magazines they had fortunately brought with them. After a couple of hours or so, on raising her eyes she beheld some dozen or more native women approaching in straggling procession. This was, at all events, a break in the lonesome monotony.

"What do you want?" Perhaps it was the imperfect Sinhalese, which failed to elicit more by way of reply than a fixed stare. Cynthia summoned the cook, her unfailing resource—when sober.

"*Palyan!*" said he ("be off").

"No; don't send them away. Ask them what they want," said Cynthia.

"Come to see English Lady," was the translated answer. "Not seen English Lady never before."

"Oh! Then let them inspect to their hearts' content."

The cook grinned, and passed on the invitation. Cynthia little knew the price of it, though! The natives are so literal. They take both the inch and the ell—and the yard, and more. The women came up, one by one, always afraid of the devil behind if they walk side by side. They came in time, all of them, and gazed from the top of her (Cynthia's) *topee* to the sole of her leather shoe, then backwards, or rather, upwards. What appeared to fascinate them most were the twelve-buttoned doe-skin gloves. Their big black eyes were hypnotised by them. Cynthia set great store by these gloves. They fitted like skin, and the reason why she indulged in such extravagance in the jungle was that otherwise her arms would have been *tables d'hôte* for mosquitoes.

"They're admiring my gloves," she was thinking. "After all, there is that 'touch of Nature that makes us all akin,' even in the jungle," she went on, philosophising and humouring her feminine vanity at the same time as she stroked her white doe-skins. Still the dozen or more pairs of black orbs remained fixed upon them. It became monotonous, that gaze, after awhile—a veritable "eat-'em-up" sort of gaze.

"Ahem!" This to break the monotony. Without result, however. "Ahem! Cook?"

"I coming, lady."

"Er—ask them what they think of me?"

Now Cynthia was not a vain woman, not vainer, that is, than most; but she never imagined they'd say aught less than a queen, with those gloves on!

The Cook did as desired. The women looked at one another and spoke a few words very low, glancing at Cynthia furtively, and again rivetting that deep, fixed stare on the gloves. The Cook grinned, but was silent.

"What do they say?" asked Cynthia. It occurred to her the cook, being a young man and a bachelor, might be shy to translate a gush of admiration. And yet she was curious, very curious, to know

"Come, speak out, man," she continued, encouragingly.

"Sinhalese women say 'Lady crazy,'" he blurted out.

"CRAZY! And why, pray?"

"Sinhalese women say Lady wear clothes on hands. Lady *must* be crazy. Sinhalese women 'fraid, and ask to go."

Cynthia laughed, not too amiably.

"Oh yes, they may go—certainly."

Thereupon a babel of tongues, as the women grouped around the cook.

"What now? Tell them to be off—*at once.*" It is *not* pleasant to be thought crazy, and to be told so, particularly when you think you're being regarded as a Queen.

"Sinhalese women say they want rice-money," the cook continued translating.

"Give them rice; and there"—throwing a handful of coppers, "And tell them, *not to come again.*"

This was Cynthia's first At Home in Jungle-land; she intended it to be the last.

That night the moon rose late, and it was much quieter, so they resolved to improve the opportunity by having a good six hours' sleep. About 1 A.M., however, they were awoke by a strange commotion. Buffaloes had broken in. Luckily the moon was up. All were aroused, and ready promptly. A singular sight presented itself on opening the door: a herd of wild buffaloes careering about in the moonlight, and setting up savage and distracting bellowings. From a safe vantage it was a wonderful spectacle. Alas! No vantage of safety was there, however. Should the herd dispose to turn in that direction the whole "encampment" might be demolished. Guns and revolvers were immediately in requisition. Wild roars rent the air as shot after shot was fired. Possibly now, more from fright than fury, the buffaloes bellowed and bounded, breaking down the fence and everything that came in their way. The howling of the wounded was horrifying. But what else to do? Property, human lives were at stake. It demanded all their efforts, all the ammunition likewise to keep the terrified and infuriated beasts at bay. There seemed no limit to them too. No matter how many fell, others filled the gaps. It was an eerie, witching spectacle in the moonlight. The still atmosphere soon began to reek with the odour of blood. But the battle went on. The intention of the frenzied creatures was evidently to storm the bungalow. Desperate endeavours they made, only kept back by the volley of shot, for every one of the party, five all told, continued firing for dear life. The odds were in favour of the buffaloes all the same. Lashing their tails, tossing their heads wildly, half a dozen of them would band together to make an attack, each attack more determined, each animal more frantic than before.

Perhaps it was the excitement that kept hope burning in the human breast. More likely they realised not the peril, the terrible fate which surely must await them. No such fear, indeed, no such thought ever entered their heads. It was sport—glorious sport. Cynthia even was carried away by it.

"Stay! What is that?" For the first time she spoke, as through the smoke-charged atmosphere she beheld a large dark form moving majestically amongst the wildly careering animals, scattering and dispersing them. Colossal it looked as it wended its way, the very shots ricochetting as they struck the monster's back.

"The field-glass—*quick!*"—the air being too thick with smoke to see distinctly.

"An elephant, by Jove!" Guns and revolvers were laid low. There was something grand, almost sacred, in the way that huge creature made a path for himself amongst the bellowing buffaloes.

All held their breath as on he came, stepping over slain and expiring carcases—a veritable king of the jungle, regal, grand! All unconcerned he trod his steady way, dispersing the beasts far and wide, the buffaloes awe-stricken by the dominating presence, until it had the path to itself. Would it come *their* way, was now the thought in each human mind. Cynthia's feminine intuition answered, "No." Furthermore it told her this magnificent creature, this king of the jungle, was their protector, their friend.

"Dear old thing! Dear old Rogue," she found herself murmuring; "he has come to protect the hand that fed him." There were tears in her eyes as she strained them to watch him, this elephant, as he passed on in the moonlight—on, into the heart of the jungle, and was seen no more. The invading army of buffaloes was vanquished. Then Cynthia ought to have fainted, but she didn't, nor even had hysterics for the first time in her life. No, she had a whisky and soda instead, and afterwards went to sleep again, when all was safe and quiet, murmuring, "Dear old Rogue! He came and saved the life of the hand that fed him?"

CHAPTER XIII

"A scene worthy of a Dante!"—The jungle ablaze—The monster pursued by flames and smoke—A soul-thrilling situation — How the big boa-constrictor emerged—Better than sport.

ALAS! a piteous scene was revealed at dawn! None of the coolies turned up, moreover. The two days' pay would keep them a week, why work?

The third day, however, some of them put in an appearance. The forest land had to be burnt; no manual labour could effect that clearance. Coolies were consequently stationed at certain distances with blazing torches of rolled cocoanut leaves. At a given signal—the firing of a gun, they were to set fire to the dry and tangled branches. A swish and a roar and a magnificent spectacle was presented. Gigantic tongues of flames darted out from showers of sparks, with masses of purple smoke alternately belching forth and ascending in sunlit circles to the skies, amid a roar, a cracking and a stupendous glow. "A scene worthy of a Dante!" breathed Cynthia.

"Look! *Look!*" she cried, as from out the

rolling clouds of smoke and the living tongues of flame there emerged a boa-constrictor! Now arched to the height of a giant, now gliding along on its belly, the marks on its beautiful skin glittered in the fierce light of fire and of sun. All looked on—fascinated by the sight. For a second or two it would be hidden or be seen very indistinctly through the smoke. But anon its gemlike eyes would flash out, and its writhing, wriggling form reappear in a frantic endeavour to escape from the scorching, devouring flames. An exciting, an awful chase for life! It seemed there was purpose in those relentless flames. Like fiends they pursued, sometimes overtaking this monster of the forest. Not a word was spoken as the flight and pursuit went on. The jewel-like eyes scintillated frenziedly as the boa-constrictor sped on, the merciless flames pursuing. The heat given out by the blazing forest was tremendous. Many other creatures of the jungle endeavouring to escape likewise came out. But they were speedily swallowed up, consumed, and seen no more. Only the boa-constrictor survived. Amidst the cracking and the roar the "hiss-hiss" of the cobra was distinctly audible, besides at times the muffled moan of the huge boa-constrictor in its flight for life. Dismal was that moan! It had the death-bell tone. Once, when the fire overtaking scorched the hieroglyphiced skin, the monster reared to well nigh its full length, facing the glorious midday sun. Then hurling itself at a tree, twined around the trunk, and uprooted it in an instant. Fuel for the fire, more fuel, which only made the blaze the greater. Ah, but it—the uprooted tree stayed its progress though! There was strategy in this supplying of fuel—the wisdom of the serpent. The rapacious flames were satisfied—for a few seconds. In these few seconds depended the issue of events. The boa-constrictor, cunning, wise, took advantage of this opportunity. A few seconds only. But that sufficed. Danger was left behind. With mighty leaps and bounds, at a pace pen cannot compete with, this huge creature coursed over and under the undergrowth, through the branches, many of which were broken and flung aside, its great coils diminishing, the flash of the glittering eyes becoming rarer and rarer, until the monster was lost in the distant jungle. Not a trace of him now, nor ever again was seen.

"Why didn't you shoot him and get his skin?" has been the first and frequent question asked by Europeans at home.

No. There are times when the keenest sportsman hesitates. This was one of them. The grandeur of the scene, together with the desperation of the situation verged on the sacred. Cynthia would as soon have shot her darling "Rogue"—almost!

CHAPTER XIV

A queer creature: Was it a blue-faced gibbon?—Human heritage: woe?—Cynthia envies the mischievous, merry monkey—A sanguinary stream—How they lost one of the little bulls—A gargantuan maw—"Hardup!" What should they do?—Mohammedan kindness—"There's no place like home."

IT was trying, wearisome work superintending the coolies. Monotonous also for Cynthia, alone on the verandah, particularly when the magazines were exhausted. "Have it done by contract," she suggested for the nineteenth time, when, next morning, not a coolie put in an appearance. It seemed likely to be a case of Hobson's choice.

"Cheer up. The matutinal tub awaits. Come!"

What would the ladies of King's House have said if they had seen Cynthia in pyjamas showering the water from a *calabash* over her curly flowing locks in the middle of that crystal clear stream?

"Cheer, boys, cheer; no more of idle sorrow," she sang between whiles. There was no one to see, no Mrs. Grundy (a pity that), for the rainbow-coloured jacket was very becoming to delicate, transparent skin. European ladies become like wax dolls after a few years' residence in Ceylon owing to anæmia. The water was cool and delightfully refreshing. But as she raised the replenished *calabash* and with it her regards she espied—*an object*. What was it? A gibbon? a blue-faced gibbon come to join in her song, for a certain species of this monkey *does* sing? No; this was too tall for a singing gibbon: they are small creatures. What was it? Dark-brown in colour, innocent of clothing, a head covered with a tangled shock of black hair, partially covering the face also, from out which two bright but frightened-looking eyes peered and for an instant met her own. "A Vedda! by all that's wonderful!" A flash of flat feet and he was gone! Back to his home in the jungle, never to emerge again, terrified may be by the vision of an *Englishwoman in pyjamas!* The lasting impression left on Cynthia's mind was the sad melancholy of the countenance beneath the temporary fear. Upon mentioning this to an ethnologist afterwards, she was told this melancholy is the chief characteristic of the aborigines of Ceylon. They *cannot* laugh nor smile, never having had occasion for either. And yet, how jolly are the monkeys! Is this our *human* heritage—woe?

"If I *am* to be reincarnated," philosophised Cynthia, "let me be a mischievous monkey; not a singing gibbon, but a——"

Photo. Plate, Ceylon

A GROUP OF VEDDHO (ABORIGINEES OF CEYLON) WITH BOWS AND ARROWS, IN THE JUNGLE. ONLY SOME THIRTY NOW ARE EXTANT. THEY HAVE NEVER BEEN KNOWN TO SMILE

'What's the meaning of this?" Her soliloquies were interrupted by the stream's clear water becoming ruddier and ruddier. At a few hundred yards' distance the little bulls were likewise taking their morning tub. Now as Cynthia traced the stream's change of colour away yonder, she saw one of the bulls sink, sink beneath, while the water became still ruddier. Then arose what looked like a big coral reef, only that it had jaws that opened and closed, while red blood poured from an awful maw. With a shriek she was out of the stream and calling—Help! But alas! too late. One little bull had fallen a victim to that gargantuan maw, one of its hind legs being entirely bitten off, while the body sank into a watery grave.

Of all their experiences this was the worst. The crystal streamlet was turned into a streamlet of blood. In a moment a halter was procured and the other bull rescued and drawn out. No more tubbing in that stream! Never again! the idea was too horrible.

"It might have been the Lady," said the Cook, whose notion of consoling was to pile on agony.

"It's quite bad enough, Cook, for with all his little caprices he was one of us," was the reply.

They were only "little caprices" now, poor little bull! That awful crocodile!

But the Cook had been called away in the midst of breakfast preparations. Upon their return—a solemn one—they found robbery on a wholesale scale had been committed. Not a tin of any sort of provisions was left! Yet, not a trace of any of the marauders. Where *could* they have got to? Where *had* they come from? Ah, this was the land where slight of limb as well as sleight of hand is an inheritance. Looks were exchanged—in silence.

"Hard up!" said the *minah*—opportunely.

This evoked roars of laughter. It *was* so *apropos*.

"Hard-up, indeed!" echoed Cynthia.

"What shall we do?"

"Go home?" Cynthia, up to now, had never been known to show the white feather!

"Can't, with only one bull," was the reply.

"Snipe," suggested Cynthia—for with all her horror she was hungry—pointing upwards.

Bang, bang, bang! Snipe in plenty. Then there was bread fruit, and *jak*, and yams . . .

"Oh, we'll fake up a breakfast fit for a queen. By the way, I wonder how ye native likes our Paysandu tongue, Bologna sausage, mock turtle soup, foie gras—Oh—ooh—oh! Never mind! here cometh Cook with breakfast—*houp là!*"

This, some half hour later. Cynthia, rising from the inverted *chattie*, had need of all the good spirits astrologers ascribe to her as a native of Jupiter. When she looked for knives and forks wherewith to eat the impromptu *déjeuner* not one was visible—all had gone in the burglarious raid. It might have been a "scratch" repast; it was not without its touch of humour and merriment all the same. And, as Cynthia's philosophy had it, "Did it not betoken a climax to the bad luck?" There is, in nature, a universal ebb and flow: when things reach their worst—wasn't this the worst, to be stranded minus provisions, minus means of obtaining them in an unknown, uninhabited spot in the jungle? The situation was original at any rate. Wouldn't it afford a splendid opening chapter to a thrilling romance—a penny novelette?

The elopement of a wildly romantic young couple—an earl, of course, and—no, not a poor but pretty governess, earls have better taste now-a-days—a Gaiety girl; or, better still, a multi-millionairess disguised as a daring *chaffeuse*, dashing out of sight of Society, keen on exchanging all its shams for the "simple life" of the jungle. So Cynthia's imagination run on, keeping all amused. Suddenly she stopped.

"S—sh! Dinna ye hear?—*Wheels!*"

All stood at attention—Cook included.

Wheels sure enough—out on the road.

To the fore, with flags! It *might* be Jacobis returning! Pyjamas were hoisted and flourished frantically, with the result that the cart was seen to turn in the direction of the stranded.

Lopping along for a while it then pulled up and the occupants, two men, Moslems, judging from their conical straw hats and clean shaven heads, were seen to alight. Gathering their *kambayas* around them to keep free of the briars, and exposing a length of limb in a charmingly natural manner, on they came, picking their way through the undergrowth of jungle. When near enough to recognise with the naked eye—for the field-glass was part of the plunder—

"The Mohammedans!" was the dual exclamation.

A minute later, "*Salaam Mahatmaya: Nona Salaam*," was the greeting, touching their foreheads with their finger tips.

Cynthia was in no mood for *les convenances*. She plunged into a recital of the circumstances of the situation, their pitiable plight, instanter.

Wanting provisions? Their (the Mohammedans) cart was well stored, for they were journeying far.

All was at the *Mahatmaya's* disposal.

The superintendent—was he not here? they asked.

The superintendent took himself off the night of arrival and had not returned, they explained. At this the Mohammedans exchanged looks and smiled. Cynthia knew that smile.

"Do you know anything of him?" she asked.

This brought forth the following tale. The

man, Jacobis, had not been on the estate for months, no nearer in fact than the Rest House, where wages, coolie hire, &c., awaited him on the third day of each month. With this he had purchased a small property near his native village, where, with two women whom he had taken to wife he was living contentedly, at his master's expense. The story of his heroic encounter with wild boars had been evolved from his own imagination.

The leg wound, however, was reality, having been acquired in training his own bull. The wound had healed, the Mohammedans had been informed; but upon hearing the *Mahatmaya* was coming means had been resorted to re-open and irritate the wound afresh, in order to exempt him from walking and work, in addition to exciting sympathy and gaining a reward for his heroism and sufferings; all of which had been crowned with glorious success.

Why had they, the Mohammedans, not told this before?

They thought this was the object of the master's visit, to inspect and make other arrangements; likewise that the man Jacobis had already been discharged, the fact of their not seeing him the night of the moonlight call helping to confirm this idea, and that another superintendent had taken his place.

"The rascal!" ejaculated Cynthia, "Don't you remember how he remained in the cart on that occasion, our moonlight call, his leg more than usually painful, as he declared? Oh dear! virtue is indeed its own reward in this wicked world, for 'divil a bit is there any other.'"

The Mohammedans were full of sympathy and willing to give any and all assistance in their power. It was hard but—*Kismet!*"

"Yes, and *Kismet*, your coming this way," answered Cynthia. This pleased them. They *salaamed*, they beamed. "If you could spare us one of your bulls now," she went on, improving the opportunity as tactful woman best knows how. Another gracious *salaam* from each. A bull should be sent at sundown. Meanwhile, would the lady permit her cook to go to the cart and select what might be required in the way of provisions for the rest of the day and the forthcoming journey? What *Christian* could do more?

The Mohammedans' word was kept. By 6 P.M. the caravan was equipped. By 8 P.M., when the tars were shining brilliantly, they commenced their homeward journey.

"So much for our gipsying in the jungle!" said Cynthia. "After all, there's no place like home.'

CHAPTER XV

A strange experience of an opium den—How the different races are affected—"Chinaman glory in tears"—A Tamil tom-tom beater runs amuck—The greatest surprise of all.

THE night was in keeping with the occasion—dark, notwithstanding the fact of millions of stars that shone with wondrous brilliancy from out that purple-black dome. It was a drive of some hour and a half in a country-hackery (being the least conspicuous) along the dusty, hot high road. At about 11.30 the *hackery-wallah* pulled up at an ordinary *caddy*, whence, although shut up at this late hour, issued a pungent aroma of *chilis*, tempered by others less invigorating. The *caddy* was a detail, or, more correctly, a day-time adjunct of this *cadjan* and *wattle* erection. As a matter of fact it was an opium den. A screen of plaited cocoanut-leaves, which by day was raised and supported on a couple of poles, now hid the entrance. A gentle tap, however, immediately elicited a response, the occupants of the hackery being expected. Nevertheless, the only preparations apparent were the two rush-bottomed chairs, one at each edge of a *tattie*. This *tattie* being a trifle too narrow, revealed a glimpse on either side of an inner apartment. When Cynthia took her seat she found she had a support for her back in the trunk of a cocoanut-palm, which towered through the roof to the height of about eighty feet. But behind the *tattie* the midnight drama was about to commence, in that ill-lit, badly ventilated apology for a room. Already a dozen or more "natives" of different nationalities and castes were assembled, caste being on these occasions sunk in one common brotherhood. This company was continually being supplemented, and each new-comer seemed to gravitate to his own place, be it a seat on a low "string bed" covered with dingy drapings, or the mere cow-dunged floor. The garish glare of wicks afloat in cocoanut-oil showed up a very fair-sized apartment, bare, with no attempt at decoration or comfort. A couple of attendants—Sinhalese—moved about, each carrying a copper plate or dish, the one containing smouldering embers, the other pipes, cups of black coffee, little mounds of leaden-coloured sticky-looking stuff, tobacco, and a long needle. No sooner did a new-comer enter than the attendants approached him with these offerings. If a pipe were taken a small quantity of tobacco was put in in the usual way, then with the needle a little of the thick treacle-like compound of one

Photo. Plate, Ceylon

THE STREET BETWEEN DEHIWALLA AND BAMBALIPITIYA ON THE WAY TO MT. LAVINIA, GIVING A VIEW OF A HINDŪ TEMPLE AND A NATIVE SHOP, USED AT NIGHT AS AN OPIUM-DEN

of three different sorts—opium, mixed with *bhang*, or with *gungah*, or *hasheesh*. This on the needle was heated over the red-hot embers, then blown upon, and a *mantram*, or charm, muttered over it. This done, the opium, with *bhang*, *gungah*, or *hasheesh*, by means of the needle was probed into a little hole in the pipe's bowl; another *mantram*, whilst steadily and fixedly gazing into the contents of the pipe, then placing the stem in the mouth, a few "draws" (the number varying according to the temperament), and the smoker passes into oblivion of all material surroundings. The pipe appeared the most popular. Those who chose the coffee (in which, of course, were the same ingredients) manifested restlessness, and in some cases half a dozen cups were drunk ere peace possessed the drinker. Some there were who, ignoring both pipe and cup, took the opium with the tip of the little finger and swallowed it thus. This seemed the most expeditious. The "den" by midnight was packed. The cow-dunged floor was carpeted with brown beings of all shapes, sizes, and shades—all in *demi-toilette*, while the "string beds" and Singapore lounges were alike crowded. Those who wore anything around the throat—an *Appoo* (head-servant), for instance, brave in a fine linen shirt of his master's—took the precaution to loosen it, as also all who wore a turban or the head-comb divested themselves of it, although at any other time not for a consideration could they have been induced to do so. That head-comb marks *Vellala* caste. The features of one man when the turban was laid aside appeared to be familiar to Cynthia; more and more so as she strained her eyes to see until convinced. Then: "Our *Muttu!*" she murmured beneath her breath, for even then she could scarcely credit the evidence of her visual senses. It was a new *Muttu* they had recently got, a *young* man *with* his turban, bald and quite old *without*—the new *Muttu* nevertheless. One must be prepared for surprises in the East—Ceylon is a land of them. It was interesting to observe the different effects on the different nationalities, for be it remembered there are thirty-six different peoples in India alone. A Sinhalese of *Vellala* caste, albeit combless now, a good-looking man, well-groomed, and with large dreamy eyes and splendid teeth, notwithstanding their dazzling whiteness was stained by "betel" chewing—in less time than it takes to tell, *he* was "off." Still as a corpse, except for an occasional twitching of the muscles and slight uplifting of an eyelid when nothing but the white was visible. A figure in stained marble or in bronze could not, but for these little convulsive movements which soon abated, a statue could not have been more serene. A Malay, on the other hand, was very restless;

either his brow ached or was heated, presumably, by the way his hand pressed it. He tossed about on the floor, muttering incoherently to himself. Evidently fearing that he should disturb with his one-sided argument, the attendant came and gave him a poke with his big toe, a most useful member of the human body to an Oriental. This having no lasting effect, with his own dirty little finger the attendant administered another dose of the sticky compound, then, with a kick, turned and left him —pacified now.

A Chinaman soon dropped his pipe, and, hugging his knees, commenced weeping, genuine tears filling his almond-shaped celestial eyes; these the attendant sympathetically wiped away with the shedder's long blue-cotton sleeve. Apparently this Chinaman's was "the luxury of grief," for he went on weeping, always with a bland, broad grin on his countenance.

"Chinaman alway do so," the proprietor obligingly explained. "Chinaman glory in tears."

All was strangely silent now. Strangely weird, too, were the shadows cast by the gestures of the occupants of that inner apartment. The narcotics, perhaps, were in the air, for the scene seemed so visionary, so unreal. Even the most prosaic might have found it difficult to preserve their normal faculties. It was dazing, stupefying.

Suddenly, however, a long, loud shriek dissipated the soporific silence.

A tall and handsome Tamil of *Berewayo*, or tom-tom beater caste, had risen, and was striking picturesque but by no means *un*alarming attitudes. What a figure for a tragedy! His immense black eyes flashed fire all round. One bronzed arm was uplifted. But not before the bony fingers had taken a knife from the loin-cloth. The uncovered limbs made attempts to stand erect, many attempts, and failed. Then another effort and the man was up, swaying though, as he brandished the knife and continued declaiming.

"Tamil-man run amuck. Lady have no fear," said the proprietor, reassuringly, and motioning to the attendants. Immediately a brazier containing smouldering embers, on which powdered narcotics were thrown, was held beneath the Tamil's nostrils. The threatening gestures subsided, the knife fell to the ground, the whole body became limp, while those black orbs gradually lost their fire, their anger.

He sighed, and would probably have fallen had not the two attendants—for the Tamil was a big man and heavy for an Oriental of his caste—supported and led him out into the cool air of early morning.

Cynthia thought they had better follow suit. A ten rupee note elicited *salaams* and smiles galore from the obliging proprietor, who himself undertook the awakening of the *hackery-wallah*—no insignificant undertaking. Cynthia thanked the stars shining brightly still above her when she found herself outside the "opium den." It had been a night of experience, but the morn brought the greatest surprise. Upon opening the *jalousies* at 7.30 there was the Tamil, the run-amuck Tamil, atop of a ninety foot high cocoanut palm leisurely plucking the nuts, seemingly in no wise worse for his night out.

CHAPTER XVI

The Portuguese Ceylonese: interesting people—Cynthia receives an invitation to a *Strom-strom*—Cynthia accepts—Poor Mrs. Grundy!—The *Fandango*, the *Strombello* at their height—A scene of revelry by night—The monsoon bursts—A sodden, satin train.

IT was on the platform of the Dehiwella railway station one evening that Cynthia first saw and heard a company of swarthy-complexioned—not olive nor cinnamon-brown like the Sinhalese—musicians making merry with fiddles—violins would be a misnomer—guitars, castanets, tambourines, and other queer-shaped, oddly stringed instruments. The effect was fascinating.

"Who are they? Not lethargic Sinhalese, surely?"

"Oh, no; descendants of the Portuguese—merry fellows and born musicians—all relegated to the mechanic class here now," was the answer.

"Interesting," said Cynthia, recollecting that prior to the Dutch, Ceylon had been in possession of the Portuguese. "I wonder if they still dance the strombello, the fandango, and the bolera? I'll ask"; and in less time than it takes to tell the question was put, Madame Grundy!

The swarthy faces, with passion-lit eyes, softened with smiles. Yes, they could dance the fandango, &c., &c., and by way of establishing that fact the musicians not only struck up, but the entire company commenced to execute, with ever-increasing *allegro* step, the opening figure of the *fandango.*

The Colombo train came in just then, bringing its contingent of British who reside in pretty bungalows here by the sea. These British manifested their superiority in their accustomed way —with a hard stare. Nevertheless the fiddling went on, with the occasional clash of cymbals, rattan and jingle of the tambourine, twanging of guitars, and click-clack of castanets, in addition to the graceful gyrations of the dancers.

" Bravo ! "

Now much of Cynthia's happy life had been spent among Austria's Old Nobility. Perhaps from them she had acquired a certain " manner." The proud nobility of Austria are exclusive in the extreme—little changed from the age of feudalism, one might say. All the same, the noble of Austria may and does meet the mechanic, the peasant, with a freedom the unbending and often snobbish British would not dream of. There are two reasons for this : one, the Austrian noble of ancient lineage and *pure* descent can afford it ; the other, the classes below never take advantage, never ape, never encroach. Had these mechanics, Mrs. Grundy, been of your and her nationality, Cynthia might have held her *nez retroussé* in the air. As it was she clapped her hands—6¼ gloves, if you please—and exclaimed, "*Bravo!*"

"Would the English Lady like to witness a *Strom-strom?*" This question was asked when dance and music ceased. If so, a *Strom-strom* extraordinary was to be held in a bungalow at Slave Island on Friday. They would feel honoured if the lady and gentleman would attend. A bow worthy of a toreador or of a brigand chief was the graceful finish to this little speech.

"At what hour?"

Nine o'clock.

Half-past nine on Friday night found them seated in their Stanhope *en route* to Slave Island. The atmosphere was dense with heat, the long-expected monsoon seemed never to come. Already upon their arrival they found a large company assembled. The ladies wore much velvet and lace, their gowns cut *à la Européen.* But it was Lisbon, not London, or rather a scene from some outlying town near the mountains *en fête*—a bit of the Pyrenees dropped down from the skies, as Cynthia averred. Whatever it was, it wasn't Sinhalese. There were symbols and pictures about betokening Christianity, for all these good folk are Catholic. The opening dance was ending, the ladies unfurling their fans, big and black and gold. Faces beneath mantillas and blossoms of frangipanni beamed a welcome. All rose to curtsey. Such ease, such grace ; were they indeed but mechanics ? Yea, verily, for did not one now stepping forward to escort the visitors to seats afterwards make Cynthia a pair of shoes for which she paid five rupees ? To a student of ethnology these people are very interesting. Zola attributes everything to heredity. If not everything, there is much in it.

Generations under tropical climatic influences may, *must*, adapt some traits ; moreover, there is the mixture of blood, that *must* out. Notwithstanding, these people are a people to themselves in Ceylon. The Portuguese proper might not quite recognise them now as their own, any more perhaps than would the Scotch those sandy-haired *gamins* with "black" faces who clamour for cents from their pure-blood brethren—poor little outcast, half-caste souls, nobody's children !

But the *Strom-strom.* The strombello now was at its height to the clash of cymbals and frenzy of fiddles. A wild whirligig waxing faster and faster until it ceased—suddenly ceased. Then a *gavotte* was danced very gracefully by a blooming young woman with red blossoms in her black hair and a swain in a suit deserving of a *matador*, the former a clever little seamstress with the unmistakable air of the *coquette* and a witching smile which she wisely bestowed on her partner—her betrothed, once in a while only.

The funny man—there's always the funny man at a party—was Punchinello. His upper storey may best be likened unto a plum pudding, a very rich one at that; the middle and lower effected a compromise betwixt Court dress and a Golliwog. Every gesture was a joke, every glance a comedy, his whole personality radiated hilarity, while the clap-trap of his lengthy *sabots* on the cemented floor was musical accompaniment and setting to his screaming comicality.

It was excessively hot, but nobody appeared to mind that. They drank cup after cup of steaming hot coffee, mostly "black," smoked cigarettes and ate sweetmeats fried in oil.

Perhaps the prettiest of all was the minuet, danced by a quartette, men and girls alike wearing long wide sashes of soft Indian silk, red, orange and green, the girls as *sari*, the men as *cummerbund*. These they waved and handled very gracefully to the rhythm of the motion, which motion was poetry in itself. Languorous, dreamy was the accompaniment, the dancers seen only through the mists of rising clouds of incense lending to the visionary effect. Almost indeed mesmeric was the effect, the music so low, the *tableau vivant* so hazy, so dim, so dream-like.

Silence, moreover, except for that soft, slow music, soothing, hypnotic; and a vision, veiled and sensuous of colouring subdued, and grace and beauty, held some charm, some spell.

But—what was that? All on a sudden a fierce wild shriek that seemed to rend the night, the heavens from end to end; then a roar, reverberant, a crash and a swish—the mighty monsoon had burst!

Every one started. Every one rose. Fortunately the dance was ended. And now the entire bungalow was alight with fitful, forked, intermittent glare—the glare of flashing fork lightning. Then again the entire dwelling shook with the roar of thunder, seemingly of a volley of cannonade, and again and again the whirlwind swish—sw-is-sh of the drenching rain.

The mighty monsoon had burst—at last.

The news went round in the brief, very brief intervals, for at other times the noise was pandemonium, no human voice was audible. It was another world. All in a moment, all found themselves habitants of another world. Doors, windows, had perforce to be closed, otherwise they would have been banged off their hinges. In spite of this, gusts of fresh air forced themselves within, chilling the perspiring occupants of the room to the very marrow. And yet, how refreshing it was! Everything within now reeked with damp; in half an hour it would be mildew. Cynthia wondered how they should get home. The phaeton had been left drawn up under a big banyan tree. How fared it with the mare and the *Muttu*? Such force would surely be spent—for a time at any rate. In this assurance they drank the steaming hot coffee, gladly now, and waited.

Closely the company sat side by side, in twos mostly, the noise so tremendous without, this close proximity was compulsory—to be heard—Punchinello earnestly gazing into the timid eyes of a pretty little lace-maker; by way of reassuring her, he doffed the comic Punchinello to assume the pensive Romeo. All in twos they sat about, silent, save for the language of the eyes. At last a cessation—temporary it might be. They had better avail themselves of the chance. The *Muttu* presumably was of the same opinion, for the crunch of wheels outside, *labouring* along and making deep ruts, announced the Stanhope phaeton.

Bows and smiles, and the company arose.

"I thank you for a very pleasant evening," said Cynthia, extending her hand to the gay and festive shoemaker, looking like the climate now, clammy and limp. Clammier, limper, though, was the *Muttu*, while the well of the phaeton *was* a well! Cynthia stepped in with white satin shoes; she descended at her verandah with something like brown paper swaddings about her feet.

The monsoon burst again ere they reached home. *How* they managed *ever* to reach home remains a mystery to this day. Beneath an avalanche from top of the phaeton-hood they *did* emerge however, Cynthia dragging a heavy weight behind—her sodden satin train!

CHAPTER XVII

A *Tambie* (Moorman hawker) calls—Cynthia rejoices when he tells her he'll bring her a good cook—Cook comes: queer in aspect, but a treasure!—Revelations of a peculiar order in the kitchen—A pedant compelled to return to earth as a humble Tamil cook—Dictionaries—A bibliomaniac in dictionaries.

CYNTHIA was sad. The cook—an Indian from Tutticorin—who had been with them throughout their gipsying in the jungle had given notice to leave. Regretfully, he declared, as he had a very kind master and mistress—gratitude that is somewhat rare from the servants in Ceylon, for the native Sinhalese are *not* by nature responsive to kindness, while the Hindoo immigrants are for the most part the discarded "black sheep" and ne'erdoweels of India. This one, however, had proved himself both honest and willing: and now, when circumstances compelled his leaving to join his brother in cultivating a cocoanut garden their savings had recently purchased, he seemed and *was* truly regretful. Moreover, he was grateful. This is why Cynthia was sad. Where should they get another cook equally as good? The breakers breaking on the coral reefs on the coast of beautiful Mount Lavinia, answered "Where?"

Cynthia, stretched on a cane lounge on the verandah, was scribbling in pencil her latest woe to her friend in Austria—the two dogs, Punch and Sprite, beneath. Presently a growl from Punch, a growl developing into a bark, in which Sprite joined.

"Only a beggar!" thought Cynthia, going on with her scribbling, knowing full well the beggar would make for the kitchen quarters.

"Lady liking buy books, newspaper?" came a voice—the voice of an itinerant *Tambie* (Moorman hawker). The choice in literature is certainly not extensive in Colombo. Londoners would say indeed it was limited. Cynthia purchased a stale copy of a sixpenny journal for a *rupee*, after which, observing that the *Tambie* was an intelligent man and well groomed, as Mohammedans invariably are, she broached the question uppermost in her mind. Did the *Tambie* happen to know of a Tamil cook?

The Tambie did—an honest, excellent man.

"Bring him, and I'll give you a *santosum*," said Cynthia relieved—jubilant.

"Later on that same day the *Tambie* returned with the man. Grey-haired, elderly—"all the better, more staid and reliable," thought Cynthia, taking all round mental notes, for she had been long "out" now.

A pair of remarkably intelligent eyes, restless rather, lean, in fact a mere backbone of a man. "Brains predominate" was the mental summing up. Good.

"Can you make good soup?"

"Yes Lady, very good soup."

"Cook fish properly? Make good curry? an *entrée?* a *soufflé?*" &c. &c.

"Yes, Lady, very good" to all, to which he had the Tambie's endorsement, "This man good cook—Lady, very."

"You'll do. Go to the kitchen and begin to prepare the dinner at once. This is your luggage, I presume?" pointing to a box left outside the verandah.

"Yes, Lady, my luggage. I go 't once."

"And tell Cook—the other cook—he may go now—when he is ready. Dinner at eight, mind."

"*Salaam*, Lady."

Cynthia heaved a sigh of relief, and passed three *rupees* on to the *Tambie*—his *santosum.*

Before driving to the Secretariat that evening, Cynthia thought it well to look in at the kitchen —this outrage on the customs of the country had long been her habit. Ceylonese kitchens are not remarkable for their illumination. It was a full minute ere Cynthia made out the figure of the new cook—it was divested now of the white jacket, consequently was less distinguishable in the gloom. At the end of the long stove he sat; to be correct, he was asquat on top of it, turban-less, with only a loin-cloth as covering to his brown withered body. At first Cynthia mistook him for a decayed branch, for fuel set up there. But that there was a human being present, she was assured by the droning, monotonous and minor, that was going on.

"The *Vedas*," Cynthia paused to listen. No, not the *Vedas* not Sanscrit at all. What was it?"

"Epi-cur-ism: the science of lux-u-rious living, Epi-glo-tis: a car-til-age which pre-vents food from enter—"

"Cook?" The call had to be repeated.

Then, with a leap like unto a fore elder of the jungle, the "withered branch," wearing a wild shock of hair at top, sprang to the ground, getting within a coat, cloth and turban in less time than it takes to tell.

"Lady calling?"

"Yes, I came to see if all were right for dinner. Ahem! What are you reading?" *Walker's Dic-tion-ary!* 'Very instructive. But—dinner at eight, mind."

With this the new cook was left to his duties.

"Evidently a very superior man," commented

his mistress. "How lucky I asked that *Tambie!* No more quarrelling over the *Ayah!* Our worries are over." With a flick of the whip oft started *Mascotte* for the Fort.

Dinner that night was a dream.

"If I see that *Tambie*, I'll double the *santosum*," said Cynthia while taking their coffee in the moonlight on the verandah.

"Better wait," was the reply.

Next day the *Tambie* did reappear, emerging from the kitchen, his mouth full. He *salaamed*, "Lady wanting book, newspaper?"

"No; but I wish to thank you for bringing the cook—here's another *rupee* for you. He's a treasure."

Some few days later, on taking the bazaar account, there was a deficit, some seventy-five cents deficit. The contents of the tray containing the market purchases for the day being gone through again and again carefully, the summing up remained the same.

"Seventy-five cents short, Cook."

Cook turned his pockets inside out. His face was innocence itself, suspicion was out of the question. It was hot and irritating work this study in arithmetic, the thermometer at 100 in the dining-room.

"Boy! Punkah! Wake up," cried Cynthia, when the *punkah* ceased swaying.

"Dear me! Well, perhaps you'll remember by and by: if you haven't lost it."

"I not lost, Lady," still looking about and feeling in his pockets, the picture of innocence. "I very sorry, Lady, very. I make 'pology—humble 'pology." Then *sotto voce*, "To 'pologise, to make 'xcuse for." Aloud: "I most particular man, honest, account correct, Lady find 'lway. Lady counting wrong, not?"

"Certainly not. There is seventy-five cents wanting, and—it must not occur again." In answer a murmur, "Occur, to happen, to come about."

Cynthia stared: she could not help overhearing, "What an extraordinary man!" she was thinking—"so original!" But aloud she said, "That will do. Remember next time; as I told you when engaging, I am very particular. Now go. And—tell the *punkah* boy he *must* not go to sleep. I have some literary work to do."

"Lit-er-ary work do" came like an echo, but two black eyes blazed from out that withered nut-like face. "Lit-er-ary work do" was repeated as after a *salaam* the little shrivelled old Tamil tottered away.

On the return that evening from a long, long drive, the dinner-gong was a long time sounding. No explanation being given by the *Appoo*, Cynthia went to the kitchen herself. Again on top of the stove was what looked like a withered branch. It now assumed a still more weird, not to say uncanny appearance, in the flickering light of wick afloat in cocoanut oil. The fires, all three of them, were out. A low monotonous droning was the only sign of life. "A witches' kitchen with a vengeance," was the thought in Cynthia's mind. The fitful, sickly glare fell full on a pair of wild dark eyes, restless, yet full of intelligence and abnormally lustrous, eyes like flash-lights flashing from a tangled jungle of grey-black hair; one long scraggy arm held a book in hand, if hand it could be called, it resembled most a claw, while a quivering, cracked voice muttered in monotone what sounded something like French.

"Cook!" Cynthia was wanting her dinner; time *was* of account. "*Cook!*"

Down descended the "withered branch," scrambling into clothes. Then, in full dress and dignity, made a *salaam* and reply:

"Lady, I attend" (*sotto voce*), "Attend, to fix the mind on, to heed, to hearken to"—"Lady wanting? Lady *de-sire*?" (*sotto voce*), "Desire, to wish for, to want."

"Dinner—of course!" Cynthia was in no mood for speculating, trifling: she was one-idea'd at present. "It's half-past eight and—taking a step forward and overturning the Cook's 'luggage'"—"and the fires are all out and the saucepans stone cold, and—put that book down, give it to me. What on earth do you want with Nuttall's Dictionary?"—flinging the same into a corner amongst a heap of refuse already evolved to organic life, microbes in millions. "Now, go on with the dinner and let it be ready in twenty minutes. Set to at once." Cynthia took a turn in the moonlight ere she returned to the front verandah—truth to tell to cool her anger, which is easily excited in the tropics, not to mention the fact of famishing.

"It's all right. Dinner will be ready in a few minutes," she said pleasantly on her return. "Something occurred—went wrong. It's all right."

Now, singular to say, there occurred an all round rise in bazaar prices at this time—meat, poultry, rice, everything went up.

"Bazaar fluc-tu-ate, Lady;" (*sotto voce*), "Fluc-tu-ate, to rise and fall: at present rise, therefore Lady paying more," explained the Cook logically enough.

"But this is preposterous!"

"Pre-pos-ter-ous, out of all propor-tion."

"Don't repeat my words. Attend."

"Lady, I hearken, I 'tend—give heed to."

"You said that yesterday when I told you never to enter the bungalow *minus* your coat."

" *Minus*, without."

" And yet, here you are again without. It's disgraceful! Preposterous!"

" Pre-pos-ter-ous, out of all pro-portion—er——" The thin, cracked voice of the old man stopped short, then went on:

" *Salaam*, Lady, that coat dirty, *dhobie* take wash."

" Have you no other? Surely with the wages I gave you only yesterday, and the box of—of clothes you brought with you——"

" I getting other coat, Lady. Lady please 'xcuse for present, please 'xcuse."

" And meanwhile"—Cynthia had a bright idea —" meanwhile, forgetful of your *caste*, neglectful of all—all *amour propre*——"

" *Am-our pro-pre*, self-respect, vanity——"

Cynthia shrieked. In a state of pant she fled through the bungalow to the front verandah.

It was some time after, when she had regained coolness and composure, she recollected Cook had told her his late wife had been a native of *Pondicherry* and had spoken French.

Next day after breakfast, when the kitchen had been purified with *Jeyes' Disinfectant*—another queer custom of this eccentric Englishwoman—and Cook had been seen to pass through the compound—still coatless—Cynthia went on a mission of investigation. The "luggage" or "box of clothes," as the natives call it, was unlocked—open, in fact. All it required was a kick. Over it went, contents falling out. Books, nought but books. Soiled, worn, well-thumbed, falling-to-pieces books most of them: one or two, however, clean, comparatively clean, well nigh new. Cynthia with her foot brought the lot towards the kitchen door and the light. Then one by one she picked them up and read on the title-page: "Walker's Dictionary," "Webster's Dictionary," "Johnson's Dictionary," "Nuttall's Dictionary," with here and there between a foreign name, and some in languages she knew not of. English, French, Portuguese, Dutch, Tamil, Sinhalese, Sanscrit, Pali, Hindi—oh, it was bewildering the number of dictionaries, and some in foreign and strange vernacular! Cook was—what? A bibliomaniac in dictionaries. Yes, that's what he was. Useless, his services had soon to be dispensed with. But, looking back, Cynthia often wonders if his were the soul of some pedant—some prig, condemned for that self-same priggishness to inhabit the body of a Tamil cook.

CHAPTER XVIII

Cynthia is introduced to "Catseye"—*Chin-Chin* lost—A strange experience and prediction—"When blood shall flow"—The prophecy of the wonder and the sign—A gorgeous sunset.

THE *Appoo* came to his mistress one afternoon with a tale that made her eyes open wide.

Cynthia had no doubt now that that old saying, "Wonders never cease," originated in the East. She lived in a whirl of "wonders."

"How do *you* know that?" she inquired.

"Catseye saying that, lady," was the *Appoo's* answer.

"And who is Catseye? And what is his authority?"

"Catseye fakir-man, lady. Fakir-man knowing many things: *everything* fakir-man knowing. How many teeth in my Lady mouth fakir-man knowing: how many hairs on my Lady's head——

"Tush! nonsense! Well, keep a sharp look-out. It's preposterous the number of things that have been stolen of late. Most of all I valued that turkey. I wouldn't have parted with him for a hundred rupees. You know that."

THE FEATHERY BAMBOOS LINING THE RIVER WHERE IN A PILE OF STONES "CATSEYE" HAD HIS TEMPORARY ABODE

Cynthia was indeed troubled about the loss of her pet Chin-Chin. She had reared him herself. A splendid specimen of that prince of poultry he became. Moreover, Chin-Chin had become one of her bodyguard. He would follow her about the garden, had made friends with the mare—even Punch permitting of his escort—and was ever by her side when either at the piano or writing on the verandah.

One morning his mistress missed his matutinal call—a chuckle just outside her window. Since that morning no more was seen or known of Chin-Chin. A reward had been offered, but nothing came of it. Cynthia lost all hope of Chin-Chin's recovery or return.

Now, when the *Appoo* left her that afternoon his mistress sat and pondered.

"Catseye! What a weird, alluring sort of name! The name of a fakir, too!"

A vision at once had arisen before her mind's eye of that "bag of bones," that "peregrinatory bag of bones," as she had designated him, who had performed such marvellous feats and made such startling predictions.

Catseye! An uncanny name, but suggestive. How much she should like to behold the owner! Alas for this heritage of Grandmother Eve!

Next day Cynthia dexterously reopened the preceding afternoon's conversation with the *Appoo*.

"Catseye saying that, Lady, *must* be—*is*," stoutly maintained the *Appoo*, with the gravity of a wooden deity. "Catseye seeing all way, everything, every way. Catseye wonderful Fakir-man."

"Hm. Well, you know, *Appoo*, it's all nonsense, as I said before; but—I should rather like to see this man. Where is he on view?" asked Cynthia, with a condescending smile, a smile peculiarly and essentially European.

The *Appoo* smiled too. What a different smile! There are volumes in an Oriental smile.

"Yes, I should *really* like to see this Fakir. He *might* tell me something about Chin-Chin. If he did I would give him a *santosum*."

"Catseye taking no *santosum*, lady," put in the *Appoo*.

"Indeed! He *must* be a wonderful man! Well, then, I'd give a *santosum* to any one who would tell me where to find—Catseye," continued Cynthia.

Another smile flit over the *Appoo's* countenance—his dreamy eye glistened.

"My Lady like seeing Catseye; I show my Lady way. Catseye staying beside water—always beside water. Beside water Catseye staying now. Lady coming see Catseye?"

Then ensued a brief dialogue, from which Cynthia gathered that the Fakir had taken up his abode by the Kelaiyni River.

"Tell the *Muttu* to have the phaeton ready at four o'clock. I shall want you to go too."

That hour found Cynthia bound for the Kelaiyni River. She knew the way well, having already paid a visit to the celebrated Temple of Kelaiyni. It was a long drive from her home in the Cinnamon Gardens though—Mutwal being left far behind. The clock in the Fort Tower had struck six when the phaeton approached a pile of stones bearing a resemblance to ancient Druidical remains. The *Appoo* spoke to the *Muttu* and the *Muttu* pulled up.

The *Appoo* sprang from his seat on the box, and addressing his mistress, requested her to alight.

It was already approaching sunset. The air was still and hazy, and silence was over all. The river looked like a sheet of silver—a mirror in which one saw the reflections of beautiful feathery bamboos and graceful, plume-like palms. Not a breath stirred the towering cocoanuts that divide the river from the mighty ocean. Not a breath nor a sound. The air was heavy laden with heat and sunshine and cinnamon scent. Already in the sky cities, the haunts of fairies, troops of archangels, gorgeous heralds and trumpeters, with chariots of fire and regiments of horsemen, were forming, as though the battle of Armageddon were about to be fought in the heavens. Such allegories one may read in the glorious sky of Ceylon!

And beneath it all Cynthia, under the guidance of the *Appoo*, wended her way through the long prickly "love grass" in the direction of that pile of stones by the Kelaiyni riverside.

At a sign from the *Appoo* she halted. The *Appoo* uttered a cry—thrice. In answer, what looked like a dark-coloured reptile wriggled out from the erection of stones. Half-way down the body, however, was a cloth—a loin-cloth. Furthermore, Cynthia remarked that although when on the ground creeping it had the sinuous action of the snake, when the head was raised and the body erect the dignity of humanity was there. A brief colloquy took place between this strange being and the *Appoo*, after which the latter, turning, said:

"Lady, please come speaking with Fakir-man before sun go down."

Not without *some* thumping of the heart, Cynthia came forward and confronted the Fakir—that most curious of creatures human, if human he could be called. And yet Catseye was held in reverence: regarded as half holy, though known to be foul. Two great black eyes blazed out of a face wizened, fleshless, burnt almost black. Hair in long matted curls naturally black but burnt red by the sun fell down to his loin-cloth—which latter was filthy. Supernatural was the brilliance as well as the power and intelligence of those eyes. All the man's vitality was concentrated therein. Such was Catseye—the nomad, the mendicant, revered and feared alike throughout the length and breadth of India and Ceylon—Catseye, the Fakir. All hailed his coming much as an astronomer hails the advent of a comet. It was portentous some—many believed. Catseye was to them an oracle. Catseye was both a sign and a wonder.

Of a truth, as Cynthia confronted this remarkable being, above all those *eyes* she was struck with amazement. Was this a creature of ordinary human birth? with human proclivities; human liabilities? human limitations? To the last she was inclined to demur. The potentialities hidden away in those eyes might be illimitable, she was thinking. Therein appeared to be a faculty, a clairvoyance that could penetrate her inmost thought, search her very soul. Never had Cynthia beheld such eyes! Now they were upon her. A moment only. Then the *Fakir* spoke, the *Appoo* translating. A rapid *résumé* of Cynthia's life was given, commencing with the days and home of her childhood. *Every detail was correct.*

Continuing, the *Fakir* mentioned many an incident known only to herself, and ultimately referred to the loss of her pet *Chin-Chin.* Chin-Chin had been stolen. A vivid description of the thief was then given, recognised easily by Cynthia. Then the *Fakir* added. "The Lady will see the turkey again—once more—alive. But it will be when blood will flow. When blood shall flow." These words were repeated, after which, turning his great black eyes on the setting sun, Catseye bowed his red-matted head and hastily departed, back into the hole in the pyramid of stones. Another moment and the mighty Indian Ocean was transformed into an ocean of gold. The sun had set.

CHAPTER XIX

Cynthia attends a *Doladima*—A picturesque scene in a cocoanut garden by the sea—The 365 usages of the ubiquitous cocoanut—A *Kattadiya* chanting 1013 *mantras* — Fulfilment of a prediction — Cynthia's dismay.

IT was an accepted fact with the natives now that this singular English lady loved learning. Cynthia, in order to gratify this remarkable taste, always made it worth her servants' while to inform her when anything of interest was coming off—or on. Hence the *Appoo* one day:

"Lady liking see *Doladima?* Good *Doladima*, morrow, Wellawatta way. *Poya* night. Lady liking go see?"

Certainly "Lady" would.

Accordingly at 11 o'clock next night Cynthia found herself being driven towards Wellawatta. It was the first night of a new moon—a *poya* night, as the Sinhalese say—a night of shadows, ghost-like shadows, chilly too for the climate, so that the natives who were about were wrapt up in sheets, which of itself contributed to the supernaturalness of the scene.

Now a *Doladima* is a thanksgiving ceremony.

In this particular case a thanksgiving for the re storation to health of a *Vellala* caste woman, the owner of a nice little cocoanut garden. The ceremony was to be held as usual in the cocoanut wood by the sea shore. The cocoanut is the friend, the fetish, and the universal provider of the Sinhalese. In it are contained all the needs of humanity, they affirm, besides as many uses as there are days in the year. Already troops of people, men, women, and children tramped the road, whilst others drove bull hackeries—all swathed in sheets. Shadowy wraiths they looked in the mild moonlight. Their bare feet making no sound, on they went, men and boys always in front, processions of them, all bound for the same goal. "The devil follows, tracking one's footsteps," is an old belief, as well as saying. This is why the men and boys go first in the Paradise of Adam, putting their women folk betwixt themselves and his Satanic majesty—for safety's sake.

A huge concourse had already assembled when Cynthia arrived. The scene that met her was a familiar one now, bearing a strong resemblance to the one she had beheld before; only that women and children were here, and instead of the *Scarlet-tongued Kali, Pattini*, the Goddess of Chastity was most to the fore. *Her* effigy it was that now presided over the principal altar—

the *Mal Bulat Tatawa.* In front of this altar, with his face turned to the East, stood the *Katadiya*, already chanting his *mantras*, whilst *vis-a-vis* instead of the poor wild woman said to be possessed of a devil, as at the previous Devil Dance, was a buxom beaming well-dressed matron, the heroine of the occasion—she who had recently recovered from an illness ; she didn't look it as she sat there on a chair, chewing cardamoms—she who now was desirous of returning thanks to the *devas* and making offerings (*dola*—whence the word *Doladima*) to the demons. Much the same performance was gone through as before. The monotonous intoning of the *Kattadiya's mantras*, the wild gyrations of the Devil Dancers, the lugubrious strumming of the tom-toms, with alternate shrieking of reeds and savage howling of the *Netun Karaweyo.* The scene, a picturesque one in the pale moonlight, was rendered more unearthly by being beheld behind the rising clouds of incense. The gorgeous colouring was thus subdued ; nevertheless, through all this veil of incense and narcotics the flash of the ruby, the glisten of the sapphire, and the soft lustre of pearls which adorned the convalescent heroine were strikingly apparent.

Night wore on. Cynthia was not sorry when informed that owing to no evil demons opposing the *Doladima* would terminate *before* cockcrow.

About 2.30 A.M. music, chaunting, dancing, everything ceased—suddenly ceased. Silence reigned—silence so sudden and unexpected the uninitiated felt more than ever conscious of the weird scene and witching hour. The only sound abroad was the cadence of the wavelets on the shore. A few minutes' absolute silence, then a gun was fired.

"Is it over?" asked Cynthia under her breath.

"Not yet, Lady. *Kattadiya* make now sacrifice, *then* all bad devil 'way go."

No sooner said than a peculiar chuckle fell on the awe-inspiring silence.

Cynthia started, straining her eyes to make out a huge black substance now in the arms of the *Kattadiya*. The *Appoo* stared into his mistress's face. "Lady!" he said.

"I know! *It is Chin-Chin!* Oh!" Simultaneously with that cry of the English lady a long sharp blade severed the head of the sacrificed bird—*Chin-Chin, Cynthia's pet.*

"Once again the Lady will see him—when blood shall flow."

Cynthia, pale, trembling, remembered the Fakir's prediction as she rose to go.

"Blood had flown"—Chin-Chin's own.

Poor Chin-Chin! He was the sacrifice—stolen for the purpose, no doubt.

No more Devil Rites did Cynthia desire to see.

CHAPTER XX

A "master-mason" appears on the scene—Cynthia begins to understand some of the "customs of the country": not all—Her *siesta* disturbed—Crowds in the compound—A chase in the lake—A timepiece stolen—A summons to the Police Court—Then to the Supreme—How law is "dispensed" in Paradise—Cynthia's unsophisticated amazement.

ONE evening a Moorman presented himself on the verandah. He came, he said, from the landlord in order, with the gracious permission of the *Mahatmaya*, to inspect the bungalow preparatory to repairs, which, by the way, were sadly needed. The *Appoo* was forthwith told off to escort the man—a "master-mason"—round. Afterwards, with a *salaam*, the man withdrew, saying the work should be commenced next day. True to his word, the "master-mason" appeared at dawn, saying the workmen would follow. But the whole day passed with no sign of a workman. The "mason" remained, however, making friends with the servants and the dog *Punch*, and having his curry and rice while waiting—waiting in vain. Next day the same occurred, and the next. Cynthia got rather tired of it, but on mentioning the fact was told it was the "custom of the country." Oh dear! how that expression haunted her! She *could* not get acclimatised to it! She spoke to him—the "master-mason"—herself, with the result that next morning—Friday—a pail of *chunam* (white-wash) met her vision on opening the *jalousies* at daybreak. Even Cynthia had hopes now. Alas! she was growing very sceptical in the East, and yet what a golden, glorious land it was! What an Eden! By noon, however, when she went to take her *siesta*, her repose was disturbed by a hubbub in the compound and a rush of "natives" passing the window. *Punch* was up and alert in an instant, all on the quiver for excitement, yet, as ever, regardful for the safety of his mistress.

The compound and back verandah were crowded with people—men, mostly, and the loafers of the neighbourhood. What was it all about? It was difficult to distinguish the bungalow servants in the multitude; but presently a neat *Vellala* caste Sinhalese, whom Cynthia recognised as the *Appoo* of the bungalow opposite, came forward and said:

"Moorman thief—stole lady's watch—*Muttu* catch him in the lake."

This explained all eyes being fixed on the lake, which the back compound bordered. And there, sure enough, in the water was a chase going on.

The Oriental glories in sport. Their big, languid eyes glowed as they watched the chase. *Punch* also was caught by the excitement. Cynthia was dazed for the moment; then remembering her watch, chain, &c., were under lock and key, her gaze went wandering round the room until she missed a timepiece—*that* was the watch. Still the crowd increased. Voices, clamour—for bets were on. Meanwhile the swimming-chase continued, until the swimmers looked like big waterfowl skimming over the lake—the Moorman (the *pseudo* "master-mason") and the *Muttu* (horsekeeper). Useless utterly to demand their departure. The mob were in possession, notwithstanding the fact of a little Malay constable being presently added to the crowd; *he* enjoyed the sport as much as any of them. It *was* exciting. That hot mid-day sun streaming down on the golden water—the chase—the crowd, heterogeneous yet so picturesque—the gorgeous blossoms of the pomegranate, flambeau, passion, and shoo-flowers—the very atmosphere glinting all colours through the sunlit haze! At last a cry went up—the man was caught. A scuffle went on in the water; then the victorious *Muttu*, securing his prey, turned and swam back to shore. "Heigh—ho!" from the crowd in chorus, all craning their necks to get a better view. The tension after this somewhat abated, and the *Appoo* of the bungalow opposite explained to Cynthia that, being in one of the bedrooms of his master's house, he had seen the Moorman stealthily make his way into the lady's drawing-room from the front verandah. Judging from his manner the Moorman's intentions were evil, he—the *Appoo*—came out, crossed the road, entered the lady's bungalow, and caught the Moorman in the act of pilfering the timepiece, which he endeavoured to secrete but failed. Nevertheless, the timepiece was retained.

A struggle had ensued. The Moorman, releasing himself, fled through the bungalow, and there being no other means of escape, leapt into the lake. The *Muttu*, grooming the mare outside the stables, pursued. These two — the "master-mason" and the *Muttu*—had been friends all the week ; but that's a detail in the Paradise of Adam—a "custom of the country." No sooner was all explained to Cynthia than the swimmers both returned, the *Muttu* holding on to the Moorman, who was apparently in an exhausted condition. When the constable commenced to belabour him with his *bâton* Cynthia interceded. His—the Moorman's—cries were pitiable. At this juncture another came on the scene—a sergeant of police. The Moorman had been caught *in flagrante delicto*. *Nolens volens*, Cynthia must give evidence against him in the Police Court.

Many questions were put by the sergeant, a few of them being answered by Cynthia, and jotted down in a note-book, while the delinquent lay, a limp lump, on the ground. The timepiece had been dropped in the middle of the lake, and a dozen or more natives were tucking up their *kambayas* preparatory to a plunge in order to find it.

All necessary information being given, the sergeant of police, with a request that Cynthia should attend at the Constabulary before the day was over, made a motion to the constables and a "*salaam*" to the "European Lady" and retired. Then the crowd withdrew. The timepiece had been fished up out of the depths of the lake, broken, massed with mud, and taken possession of by the sergeant of police before he left.

That evening, upon alighting from the phaeton, the first thing that met their eyes in the yard of the Constabulary was an iron-barred cage, in which sat the "master-mason." Again his hands were uplifted entreatingly as they passed. The man looked so abject Cynthia was more than ready to forgive had the matter been in her power, which it was not. A full report was entered in the books, to which Cynthia's signature was attached, this formality being preliminary to the case being heard before the magistrate in the

Colombo Police Court, due notice of which would be received.

Within a fortnight that notice was received. One scorching morning found Cynthia in the witness-box in presence of the magistrate, a Scotsman. Her evidence given—and little enough there was of it—it resolved itself almost into the fact of identification of the pilfered article as her own property. The clerk of the court then rose and testified to there having been five previous convictions against the accused. "In that case," said the magistrate, "it is beyond my jurisdiction—a case for the Crown and the Supreme Court," supplementing this statement with thanks for Cynthia's presence and evidence.

Oh the heat, the stifling atmosphere, the crowd, the dust, the blinding glare of that Colombo Police Court! Bow Street is an oasis to it!

It was the height of the hot season when all Europeans should be "on the hills." Such was their programme—Cynthia needed the change sadly. She was white as wax, and her buoyant spirits were flagging with her physical health. But the Crown having taken the case in hand, she must be in readiness to answer its demands.

One week, two, three, rolled on: then one day she received the summons. Meanwhile, however, the *Muttu* had been misconducting himself to such a degree that he had been paid his wages and despatched. Somewhat awkward, seeing that he was to be one of the two principal witnesses, but—the Crown Prosecutor would arrange that, that the *Muttu* should be forthcoming.

When Cynthia arrived at the Supreme Court that torrid morning she found herself the cynosure of a thousand or more eyes, masculine orbs, all on the alert for the very unusual spectacle of a European Lady in Court. Barristers, lawyers, or advocates and proctors as they are called in Ceylon, minor officials and hangers on of the Court, witnesses connected with a murder case, loafers of all nationalities of the Orient, all shades of colour from chocolate to lemon, all sorts and conditions of clothing, with "traps" equally as varied to suit the owner's taste and means. There stood Cynthia in the midst, an English lady alone, with a thousand eyes upon her.

"I would speak to the Crown Prosecutor," she said. "Tell him, please," to any whom it might concern, and with that air of good breeding and culture that impresses and carries weight wherever it be.

Some one stepping forward requested "the Lady" to "come this way." In another minute or two she was in the presence of the Crown Prosecutor, a compatriot.

"Certainly I'll hurry the case on," said he graciously. "It will only be a twenty minutes affair. We've got the two principal witnesses—your neighbour's *Appoo* and the *Muttu*. Been discharged, has he?" he went on. "Hum! Never mind, we've got him. I'm only sorry you should have the trouble, annoyance and fatigue of coming to Court in this terrible heat. But I'll see the case comes on first, as soon as the Judge arrives. Ah, here he is!" Just then a trim little victoria and pair drove up.

This Court was certainly more airy and cleanly than the former. Cynthia was accommodated with a chair below the table at which the lawyers and barristers sat. On either side were six jurymen seated in a stall, and beyond was a daïs, in the centre of which sat the dispenser of justice in the person of the judge. The witness-box was at the left-hand side, and into this Cynthia went and was sworn.

The little she had to say she said, identifying the wrecked timepiece which lay on the table as her own property. The hero of the tragedy was in full view of judge, barristers, jury, witnesses, all, from behind the bars of an iron cage, a constable on either side of him.

The *Appoo*, entering the witness-box, gave his evidence unfalteringly and very conclusively.

Only the *Muttu's* statement was required to settle the matter. A monster *punkah* kept up a continuous draught over the head of "the Court," but its refreshing effect did not reach Cynthia where she sat. The heat was almost overpowering. Well, a few minutes more and all would be over. The Crown Prosecutor looked in her direction reassuringly.

Already some two hours and a half were spent, mostly in "red tape" preliminaries. It was now midday, when the heat is at its height. Cynthia prayed all might speedily be terminated. She was never nearer fainting in her life.

The *Muttu* went into the witness-box and was sworn, according to Tamil rites.

"Did the *Muttu* chase and catch the accused in the Colombo Lake with this timepiece in his hand?" questioned the Crown Counsel.

He did, was the reply.

"Was that timepiece the property of the English lady, his mistress—his *late* mistress," correcting himself.

He believed it was, was the answer.

"Did he suppose the same to be stolen from the bungalow by the accused?"

"No." This one word fell like a thunderbolt on everybody. The question was repeated in a somewhat simpler form:

"Did he think the Moorman had stolen the lady's timepiece?"

"No!" again, clear and emphatic.

"Why, then, had he chased the Moorman?"

"They were having a swimming match, and bets were on," was the answer.

The Crown Counsel scratched his ear with his quill and glanced at the Judge, who, however, remained immobile.

"Was this the way they spent their time instead of getting on with their work?" was the next question put, to which the reply:

"The *Muttu* had finished grooming the horse; the Moorman had no work there."

"But *that* was the reason of his being there?"

"No."

"What then?"

"To get the money the Lady's husband owed him."

"Oh!" from Cynthia. Just a corner of one of the Judge's eyes now glanced in her direction, and in that glance was a smile.

"What was the accused doing with the Lady's timepiece found in his possession? Tell the tale in your own way.

"The Lady, ashamed of the whole week having passed without paying off something of the debt, had called the Moorman into the bungalow, and while she went into her room to get some money he—the Moorman—took up the timepiece to see the time, the jalousies being closed to shut out the midday heat made it too dark to see otherwise. No sooner had he taken it in hand, than he was seized by an *Appoo*, who accused him of theft. So amazed and bewildered was the poor Moorman that, forgetting the fact of the timepiece being still in his hand, he fled and plunged into the lake, where it had been arranged the swimming-match should come off. The *Muttu*, seeing the dive, and having finished grooming the horse, plunged in likewise, and the match was started, which resulted in his—the *Muttu's* victory."

With an air of pride and triumph he told this story, and if ever truth were spoken, apparently it was now. Cynthia could scarcely contain herself. It was a relief when she was summoned to the witness-box again.

"Did her husband or did she owe, or ever owe, the accused money?" asked the Crown Prosecutor.

"No; never."

"Had he ever been employed by them?"

Again "Never."

"Was there any truth in the witness's statement?"

"Not one word."

The *Appoo* recalled, repeated what he had previously said. Then the *Muttu* again, who just as strenuously adhered to his asseveration. It was not a question of theft. It was one of chance, accident merely, the timepiece being taken up and retained in the Moorman's hand, he affirmed. A feasible tale enough. Meanwhile the afternoon dragged on. An adjournment had to be made for "tiffin." Alas! there was no tiffin for Cynthia. All she could do was to sit there in that overpowering heat, faint, worried, amazed, bewildered, the battery for all eyes, wondering and waiting until the Court should reassemble.

A long list of questions the Crown Counsel had conjured up to put to the *Muttu* and "corner" him. But an Oriental is not so easily "cornered." Spite of all he "stuck to his guns." *It was no case of theft.* He was told to "go down." The *Appoo* was recalled and gave it as his opinion—his *conviction*—it *was* a case of would-be theft. All the evidence was gone through, sifted and searched, the judge taking copious notes. Then for a time silence filled the Court, save for the scratching of quills and the creaking of the *punkah.* Hour after hour passed by. Cynthia raised her eyes pleadingly to the Crown Counsel, who himself was beginning to look fagged. Another day of it Cynthia felt she could not go through. She had not broken her fast, moreover, since early morning; then it was merely *chota hazira* (early tea). The time was approaching when the Court would rise. The Judge looked up from his scribbling and himself addressed the accused.

"Had he seen the *Muttu* since that day of the chase in the lake, that memorable swimming-match?" His Honour was an Irishman and a wit seemingly.

"Yes."

"More than once?"

"Yes."

"On friendly terms?"

"Yes."

"In the House of Detention?"

"Yes."

"Now," continued the Judge, "this timepiece was stolen from the Lady's bungalow *not* by you—by whom?"

"*The Muttu.*"

Even his Lordship's lip now twitched.

"The *Muttu* in the box again."

"*You* are accused by this Moorman of the theft of this Lady's timepiece. What have you to say?" asked the Judge.

The witness grew livid: a lurid light gleamed in his eye. The Usher of the Court had perforce to intervene, for there sprang up a hurricane of angry words blowing fast and furious betwixt the witness-box and the prisoner—not "at the bar," but in the cage: a blizzard of Tamil rhetoric that demanded all the authority of the Court to suppress. Then the witness, in injured tones, addressing the Court, said, "That man big thief.

He come to Lady's bungalow try to rob all the week. No Master Mason that—big thief—stole the Lady's clock when Lady went into her room with dog."

The learned Judge, with a glance at Cynthia, to the witness,

"So you have talked to the accused since you were discharged from the lady's service?"

"Yes, sar, much talk."

"And together you concocted this little story?"

"Yes, sar. That man d—— big thief."

The *Muttu* was too enraged to have any thought save that of revenge on the Moorman for having played him false.

"That Moorman—big thief—he come——"

But the remainder was suppressed by the Usher of the Court.

"It's certainly a clever fabrication; the jury must agree," commented the Crown Prosecutor, twirling his quill and looking relieved. The jury *did* agree. And his Lordship passed sentence of "eighteen months' rigorous imprisonment, with subsequent two years' police supervision." So the case ended.

The prisoner, between two jailers, marshalled to his cell, having to pass Cynthia, improved the opportunity by shaking his handcuffed fist in her face. No more cringing now.

The crowning touch to this, Cynthia's first

experience of a Law Court in Ceylon, was given when, sinking on the cushions of the phaeton, well nigh in a state of collapse, an arm was stretched forth, while a voice whined:

"*Santosum,* Lady, please?"

It was the *Muttu!*

CHAPTER XXI

Justice in Ceylon — The "mills" that grind both "slowly" and "exceeding small"—"Where every prospect pleases," &c.—Peter Robinson's parasol and its achievements—Worthy of *opera-bouffe*.

CYNTHIA'S first experience of a Court of Justice in Ceylon—indeed anywhere—caused her to think – fatal condition in woman! Moreover, it caused her to ask questions. Reckless of consequences as her Grandmother Eve, Cynthia's thirst for knowledge goaded her on. Men maintain that once this train is fired in the feminine mind, they are in hapless security of an express ticket to the bottomless pit. Cynthia had not, however, enlisted in the corps of "Shrieking Sisters," nor was she ever likely to. Cynthia was possessed of a mind that demanded food, as did her more material part. Likewise was she endowed with a heart that ofttimes ached at the injustice of man—not "*mere* man," mankind in the full, broad sense—and sometimes rose in rebellion and hatred of the cruelties perpetrated on the weak around her. On the verandah where, amid the profusion of tropical loveliness, the little black-eyed squirrels peeped out of the purple passion flowers, and tiny tortoises took their walks abroad, and Punch and Sprite lay stretched on guard against cobras and ticpolongas—here, sheltered from the scorching sun, Cynthia loved to sit and muse and dream. Europeans thought she must be lonely. Europeans were mistaken. Cynthia was never lonely. The gamut of her musings was wide—unlimited. The more she thought, the more there was to think, and the wider the gamut grew. From the heights empyrean to—well, perhaps the bottomless pit—everything has interest if one did but take the trouble to look for it—search it out. And even in what might seem to outsiders their monotonous life something was always occurring *worth* this "thinking out." When she sent a lengthy narration of her Law Court experience to that honoured old friend of her youth, London's late esteemed Judge, the reply she received was: "May not the Rose of Sharon blossom in the wilderness? But briars abound. Take heed lest they choke the sweetness of the Rose." But Cynthia had no desire to emulate certain *habituées* of the Courts of Law—her retired life was proof of this. Only from early childhood she had hankered after the "why and wherefore," besides inclining rather to the active than to the passive: never "Do it for me," but "I'll do it" being her refrain. Thus it was fated to come about, perhaps, that her life should be no easy one. It was interesting, nevertheless. This propensity for problems was only indulged when other material duties were done. No one could accuse Cynthia of neglect of household duties, nor of lack of taste and that finish that only a woman's hand can impart, and which, when wanting, no amount of expensive luxuries can atone for. This is essentially woman's *rôle* in the drama of life, and she who does not act up to it is no woman at all—in the true sense. Problems come after.

A new problem had been born from Cynthia's late experience. This was it. Why did not her countrymen on taking possession of the Island of Ceylon take their own law with them? The old Roman Dutch law still prevails in this British First Crown Colony. According to this antique specimen of the balance of justice, a wife can at the caprice or insanity of her husband be not only left totally unprovided for on his decease, but furthermore, deprived of her own, a wife being regarded as a mere chattel of her lord and master, which, tiring of, may be exchanged, *nolens volens*, when that lord and master chooses to transfer his affections elsewhere. Marriage under such conditions sanctioned by the law of Ceylon is either a farce or a tragedy in which the virtuous heroine —the wife—may be the victim. Withal the Union Jack of Old England waves "o'er Ceylon's Spicy

Isle"! A case in point came within Cynthia's own experience. A gentlewoman by birth, education, and social environment (in England), wife of a Civil Servant in the Government of Ceylon, was not only deprived of all portion of her husband's property at his decease but was *defrauded* of *her own exclusively*—a fact exemplifying a state of things no other civilised country would countenance. The sequel to this sad story was this. The widow of that Government servant in Ceylon, finding herself destitute, had providentially found friends—friends of foreigners in a foreign land, friends likewise of the royal rulers of her own Old England.

"A Constitutional Government," said the latter, compassionating and regretfully. "We can do nothing. It is the law, moreover; no one can interfere." After many months of waiting, during which the widowed gentlewoman might have starved, *would* indeed have starved, were it not for those friends in need, friends of a *true* "high nobility," after weary waiting and months of anxiety a pension was granted. Tennyson might have said:

The mills of " Government " grind slowly,
" And" they grind exceeding " small."

"It was written," though, as the Moslem would say, that that widowed gentlewoman was *not* to starve. Cynthia devoted many a leisure hour to thinking this problem out. Moreover, she wrote the whole narration of this cruel case of *In*justice to her friend—the honoured London Judge. His lordship's reply, a voluminous one going into details of the case, she never received. A "custom of the country"—akin to native *legerdemain.* "It was written" also that Cynthia should have another experience in a Court of Justice in Ceylon —a Police Court only this time, but deserving of narration, if only for the element of humour therein. This is how it happened.

A horse from a batch of "Walers" had recently been purchased. Now this "Waler" had to be trained to both saddle and harness, as well as to become accustomed to those native outdoor "customs of the country" which are as perplexing (when not appalling) to the equine new-comer as were the European social customs to Cynthia. For this purpose Clio, as the animal was christened, had to be escorted by the *Muttu* every morning at daybreak from the home at *Dehiwella* to Colombo, a distance of about six miles. It was usual for horse and man to be back by noon. One day, however, noon came and with it neither. At 1 o'clock, when Cynthia sat down to tiffin, she inquired again, with the same answer, "Not come, Lady." At 2 o'clock, becoming uneasy, she said, "*Appoo,* you'd better go yourself—get a hackery—something may have happened."

The *Appoo* maintained that steady, stubborn gaze of the Sinhalese which, read arightly, means non-compliance. Cynthia had been long enough "out" to know it well.

"Go at once, and you shall have a couple of rupees. Here's seventy-five cents for the hackery."

The steady gaze relaxed, there was the wraith of a smile about the mouth, moreover.

The *Appoo* went. Afternoon tea-time brought him back—alone.

"Well?" said his mistress questioningly.

"That horse, Lady, tied to tree. Sinhalese man saying not untie until Lady pay ten rupee."

"*What!*"

"That horse, Lady's horse, tied to tree," &c., &c., going over the same to simplify to European density.

"And the *Muttu?*"

"*Muttu* there, too, Lady; *Muttu not* tied to tree; *Muttu* staying with horse; *Muttu* not coming back."

"What *does* it mean?" ejaculated Cynthia.

"Sinhalese man wanting ten rupee, Lady."

"Oh yes, I understand *that* well enough."

"But *why?* How dare he keep the horse?"

"Sinhalese man *got*, Lady: Sinhalese man *keep*—'less Lady give ten rupee."

Sinhalese logic is simplicity itself, but—one-sided. A happy thought struck Cynthia.

"Why didn't *you* release the horse?"

"Sinhalese man not letting, Lady. Sinhalese man wanting ten rupee first—Lady give?"

"No, I'll be—shot if I do! I'll go myself."

"Very hot, Lady, out-door. No other horse got take carriage, no gharry 'bout this part. Lady—European Lady not going go?"

"I am; and you must go too."

Now the highway from Colombo to Mount Lavinia is one long, hot, dusty road. Picturesque decidedly, with the handsome white bungalows in large gardens on the one side and the native *boutiques* (shops) on the other, with every sort of human being, descript and nondescript, between. The Sinhalese—indeed, the Oriental has no notion of privacy—he and she, take their baths, dress, do their hair or have it done by the barber in full view of everybody. One sees the queerest sights in Ceylon.

But Cynthia that scorching afternoon was on other business bent. Men—sellers of *chatties*, fish and what not—might pause to inquire of the *Appoo* the reason for a European lady being about at that hour and *on foot;* women might come to the doorways of their cadjan huts and chatter; boys and girls might pester her for cents, "no fadder, no mudder got, Lady!" beggars might increase the tone of their perpetual drone; Cynthia wended her way—the *Appoo* following. Her loose yet becoming tea-gown held up from the dust, on she went, her parasol the only protection from the tropical sun.

Presently carriages, the carriages of Europeans, varying from victorias to buggies and dog-carts, commenced to scatter the motley yet picturesque throng of natives that always fills the road. Banks, offices had closed. Europeans were either going home or were out for their evening drive. How they looked at Cynthia! Some—and these the best bred, those really high in the social scale—raised their hats; others stared, and if they had their wives and daughters with them, the latter made some sneering remark which, however, the husband, to his credit be it said, did not encourage, but flicking the horse hastened on. Such incidents forced Cynthia to wonder if, when Bishop Heber wrote those lines—

Where every prospect pleases,
And only man is vile,

they were intended to imply to the "heathen" native alone. May be 'twas the pretty tea-gown that excited envy or derision—which? But what more suitable when the thermometer stands at 110° than a loose muslin robe? Cynthia had at any rate the courage of her opinions and acted accordingly, let Mrs. Grundy of the Colony deride as she might—or *envy!*

Wellawatte was passed; Bambalapitiya nearly, when the *Appoo*, approaching, pointed to a group assembled under the shade of a mango tree.

There was the horse, there the *Muttu*, and squatting around the animal were some three or four of the lowest caste, most ruffianly looking natives it had ever been Cynthia's misfortune to behold.

"*Muttu*," said Cynthia, drawing nearer, "release the horse and bring it home."

The *Muttu* came a step forward—reluctantly.

"Come—quick," continued Cynthia firmly.

But the group of rapscallions were up at this, their hands on the animal's halter, their voices in chorus addressing Cynthia, "Sinhalese men saying wanting ten rupee, Lady," interpreted the *Appoo*, standing at a distance, as became his high caste. Cynthia was sharp enough to detect glances being exchanged all round. Freemasonry always exists among the natives in spite of caste—until their individual interests clash.

"*Muttu*, take the horse—I insist."

But the *Muttu* made no advance. He either would not or he dared not. Useless to transfer the order to the *Appoo*. Cynthia came forward herself. Soon as her fingers touched the knot the halter fell from the tree. She was surprised at the success herself. The ruffians, infuriated, surrounded her, talking vociferously, and making endeavours to bar her way. With her sunshade, however, she kept them at bay. Afterwards she said her "good demon must have been at hand and helped," for whilst one hand was occupied with Mr. Peter Robinson's parasol, the other, securing the halter, led the horse away. A sorry situation for an English lady, but Cynthia was blessed with that priceless bump of humour—born with it. It helped her over many a stile. It helped her now. Spite of heat, fatigue, fear (if fear she had) of these low caste native ruffians, Cynthia held on—literally as well as figuratively held her own, leading the animal until, once out in the open road, she insisted again on the *Muttu* taking her place. This he did now—willingly, his mistress having proven herself, if not the stronger, at any rate the superior power. "Nothing succeeds like success" is true as it is trite with human nature, black as well as white. Thus the procession proceeded homeward. After dinner the *Muttu* was summoned to the verandah to tell his story of what Cynthia designated this "novel system of equine brigandage." It was this. While leading the animal quietly along the public higbroad, some three or four men, suddenly emerging from a side garden, seized the halter out of the *Muttu's* hand and led the horse away to a mango tree, where they secured it. Upon the *Muttu* remonstrating, the men—strangers to the *Muttu* (of course) demanded ten rupees ere the animal should be released or restored. Useless to argue, to reason, or to resist. Ten rupees or the horse remained captive.

Funny, downright funny was this.

"Worthy of French *opera bouffe*," as Cynthia said. "But—the flag of sober, serious, *just* old England waves o'er this fair isle." Herein lay the anomaly.

"But," bringing herself back to the gravity of the question, "was there no constable about?" she inquired.

"No," said the *Muttu*, "no constable 'bout."

"H'm. You may go, *Muttu*."

That evening passed merrily, as indeed their evenings always did. Cynthia made sketches of natives being kept at bay with Mr. Peter Robinson's parasol by way of illustration to her graphic encounter with "ye native brigand." The sequel to the adventure occurred a morning or two later, when they were eating their *appas* again on the verandah. A yellow Malay in blue approaching, handed an envelope, likewise blue. The contents, also blue—a summons to appear at the Colombo Police Court: "Whereas the said So-and-So did permit of his property—a horse and a man—a *Muttu* in the said So-and-So's service, to trespass on and thereby do injury to the property of So-and-So at Bambalapitiya."

"What audacity! What *men*dacity! Really life is, *must* be, comic opera in Ceylon."

Ah, Cynthia, not always. Tragedy it may be sometimes. But that's another story.

CHAPTER XXII

In the District Court—Mr. Commissioner Mulligatawny—Cynthia's hero-worship of genius—A custom of police sergeants of the country—What Sir Anthony Oliphant said of a proposed law tor perjury in Ceylon.

THE eventful day of the Police Court summons came, and found Cynthia and her husband before, say, Mr. Commissioner Mulligatawny, who "eyed" Cynthia curiously while occupied in pulling his tawny brown moustache.

This Court was hotter and more crowded than the one they had already been made acquainted with. They took their seats in the "well," while the plaintiff told his story in the witness-box. Now Ceylon is a land of surprises undoubtedly: Cynthia had digested that fact long ago. Nevertheless, she opened wide her eyes at this neat little narrative the plaintiff told.

"There's a fortune in that man," she murmured below her breath, "a mine of wealth the up-to-date story-writer would transmute into thousands. He's a genius!"

Such a hero-worshipper was she by nature she turned her glowing eyes on this low-caste native ruffian with wonder, with admiration. A genius indeed! Ere she had time to regain what might be termed her moral basis, a sergeant of police was called into the witness-box. Every word of the pretty fabrication this sergeant confirmed. In fact this sergeant had actually been an *eye-witness of the trespassing*, also of the damage done. *Now* it was that Cynthia's æsthetic fancy gave place to her sounder judgment. Seen through this—the *moral* lens—those airy fabrications, though ingenious, were false; in a word, lies. What had appealed to her as imagination was invention, base to boot.

Some questions put to this witness were answered, never directly, but in "a roundabout way" replied to, which passed, however, as satisfactory. Directness cannot be expected of the Oriental.

Cynthia no longer admired. She wondered, though, still. Still more she wondered when witness after witness entering the box confirmed what had previously been stated—a crowd of them, too numerous to individualise or to particularise; their evidence all in accord.

For the defence, Cynthia called, told her story in a few words—a simple narration of facts.

Then came the *Muttu*. It was his duty to take the horse to the trainer's every morning. This he did—he "always did his duty."

"By the high road?" was the question asked.

"Yes, by the high road."

That morning, however, the *Mahatmaya* had told him to take a short cut, as the lady wanted to give the animal a trial that afternoon in the cocoanut garden. He obeyed the *Mahatmaya*—he "always did." He took "the short cut."

"Over this man's property?"

"Yes, over this man's property."

"Was any damage done to the property?"

"Yes, damage *was* done—to young cocoanuts."

The case was ended. Damages twenty rupees—with costs.

N.B.—The *Muttu* had received his "pay" that morning, together with an advance for "clothes good new for go to Court—gentleman's servant like."

The *Muttu* was seen no more.

The police sergeant would have a feast that night, a turkey may be, and ducks and chickens galore: a custom of the country.

And this is justice—justice in Ceylon!

Cynthia was forcibly reminded of the answer of Sir Anthony Oliphant—when Chief Justice of Ceylon—on being asked why there is no law in condemnation of perjury in that colony:

"Because," said Sir Anthony, "the perjured would perjure the perjurer, and the perjurer again the perjured, and so on *ad infinitum!*"

CHAPTER XXIII

Something more in Cynthia's line—Another expedition—Catholic missionary influence apparent in Mutwal — A dreamful eve—Cynthia's story whilst driving to a Hindū temple — They interview a Brahmin priest, a wise man, and hermit soothsayer in a sanctuary at sunset.

"SOMETHING in your line!"

It was indeed in Cynthia's line. A chance of becoming acquainted with a real live Brahman. This Brahman, moreover, was exceptional in that he was not only possessed of scholarly learning, but of the wisdom of the oracle.

A recluse, entirely cut off from the world, this Brahman priest had consecrated his life to the windings and workings of the world of mind, may be of soul, at any rate of super sense. The temple wherein this "wise man" dwelt was one of the most ancient in Ceylon—as old as the hill called Adam's Peak, whereon the footprint of the first man may be seen to this day on his exile from Eden. Away from the quarter of fashion, frivolity, folly; away from the track of the *gharry* passengers who globe-trot to gape at and crack feeble jokes, *very* feeble jokes, at the frescoes and friezes of an age bygone and forgotten—if it ever entered into their understanding. Go? Of course they must go.

Accordingly sunset—the first gleam of sunset—found them driving far out on the Mutwal side of Colombo. Passing through a fisher-community dwelling here, Cynthia could not fail to notice the cleanliness in comparison with others of the same caste. By way of explanation she was told that the people here are Catholics, converted originally by the Portuguese, who occupied the island previous to the Dutch.

The native descendants even now retain traits and traces of these, their first European conquerors and their missionising work. If the missionaries do no more than teach the "heathen" habits of cleanliness, their efforts should be commended. This is distinctly the cleanest and the best kept quarter of Colombo and its environs. Seen when the haze of heat is lifting to the evening breeze, the landscape is peaceful as it is pretty. Monster mahogany trees rustle their evergreen branches as on awakening from a narcotic slumber, while giant cocoanuts gracefully wave their green and golden plumes, and feathery bamboos shiver a silvery sheen, and the African palm expands, spreading out its fan-like foliage like a lady to spare her roseate blushes. The trees alone of Ceylon are worth going six thousand miles to see. Byron said:

I made me friends of mountains.

Might he not—in this Paradise of Adam—have added "and found counsellors in trees"? And ever on their left as on they drove that heaven-like eve was the ocean, not sad, not savage, languorous, low and sweet, murmuring its love song to the land. A dreamful eve in which the poet would delight, the very atmosphere seemed peopled with beings light as air; the scenery abounding with mythical creations of old-world lore. Cynthia had unearthed some of those old-time legends, when the world was not so wise as now, being herself rather a being of a bygone age than a product of the twentieth century. To while away the journey she told one those quaint old legends of Ceylon as they drove along.

Inka and Nanda

The Moon-World lay on its back and the Hare King (the Sinhalese say the *hare* in the moon, not the man) leapt out from his throne.

"A blessing the monsoon's over," said he. "I was beginning to be bored to death. Heigho!" and he yawned,—you see even a king can be bored.

"Plenty of water for the *dhobies*" continued his Majesty of the Moon. Old Sol, with his hot vulgar face will do the drying.

"Now for a turn round this little Paradise of Adam; more moonshine here than anywhere, *such* moonshine too, a paradise under our special protectorate, a garden where I love to stretch and take my gambols.

"How do, my Lord Elephant? Good even to you, Messrs. Cheetah, Jaguar, Buffalo, Jackal, Mesdames Poll Parrot, Mongoose, Cobra—all. Out for a moonlit stroll? Well, show me the way, and I'll allow my lantern to light this queer sort of world of yours." Even the elephant, lord of the jungle, looked insignificant in comparison with the Monarch of the Moon. Upon arrival at a village the first thing His Majesty saw was Inka drawing water from a well.

"Ah-ha, a pretty girl, by Jove!" said he, for though a monarch he was still a man, and all men are alike the universe over. "But her eyes are red with weeping; what can the matter be?"

The Hare King had not long to wait for an answer, for just then there came out from a *cadjan* hut a woman with a stick—a woman with a deceitful smile and an evil eye.

"Inka?" cried she. "Inka! Wasting your time weeping as usual. Bring the water. Boil the *chattie*, get the supper—quick! or may the *Rakhsi* (an evil dæmon) gobble you up alive as it surely will."

"Not so sure, old beldam," said the Hare King

to himself as he leapt into a mango tree, and made himself invisible among the branches.

"*Hakkh!* What's that black shadow in the moonlight?" exclaimed the angry woman in terror. "The *Rakhsi* for sure, come to bring bad luck. I thought how it would be," she went on gathering her *kambaya* around her and hastening into the hut for protection. "I knew something would happen when the house lizard no longer came. Inka? *Inka?*"

No answer coming to her call, and concluding her stepdaughter was busy with the curry and rice, this wicked woman crept out and stealthily crept along until she came to the mango tree. Here she stopped, took a piece of moss from the trunk, then placed in a little hole beneath a string of coral beads and a silver bangle, covering them over again with the moss.

"She'll never think of looking there, oh dear, no!" and she chuckled.

"Oh dear, no!" repeated the Hare King up in the branches of the tree, and *he* chuckled too.

"The *Rakhsi!* and with a cry she fled in terror.

Now, the supper cooked and ready to dish, Inka went back to the hut. As she went the swish-swish of the "love grass" seemed to say to her:

"Inka beware! Inka beware!
If good fortune you want, then trust to the hare."

Strange to say a shadow lay across her path in the beautiful white moonlight—the shadow of a hare. But what a big one! what a beauty!

At the same time Inka, looking upwards, beheld the moon, for all the world like a silver throne out of which the monarch had stepped.

"No hare in the moon to-night," said she. Then she fell a-wondering where her lover—her Nanda—might be. Nanda was a fisher lad, and the waves broke on the coral reefs with a moan and a groan, and Inka's heart was sad, so very sad.

"I'll bring you, Inka, a string of coral beads and a bangle next time I return," said he. That was weeks ago. Nanda lived over the Mutwal side—that was far away. He had *not* come. This was why poor Inka was sad.

"I know what I'll do," suddenly thought she. "I'll send a message by a big black crab to the Great Monarch of the Ocean, first cousin to the Hare King of the Moon. He, in his palace far out on the coral reefs yonder, will help me. Come along, crabbie," said she. All she had to do was to whisper the message and off crabbie went, glad enough; swift and sure this sea-spider went into the broad ocean. When the wicked stepmother came to the door of the hut to hurry up Inka, she was terrified at the great white spectre that seemed rising out of the ocean. So alarmed was she that she dropped the *chattie* containing her supper, which Naga, the fangless old cobra always on the lurk, immediately gobbled up.

"Help! save me! the *Rakhsi!* she'll gobble *me* up too!" cried the terrified wicked old woman. At this the Hare King aloft chuckled so heartily the whole tree shook. Meanwhile the big black crab had reached the palace of the Ocean King on a coral reef.

"What do you want, you ugly, awkward creature?" asked his gracious Majesty. The crab delivered the message, with many *salaams*, from Inka.

"Humph!" replied his Oceanic Majesty, in such a gruff voice that people thought it thundered. "I'll see to it. Be off." And the sea roared like a torrent and the wind blew like a hurricane. But it was only the Monarch breathing. The crab was glad, more glad to return even than he had been to go.

"Inka and Nanda," mused the Ocean King, "let's have a look at 'em." So saying, he breathed lightly on the ocean, and immediately the water became calm and clear as a mirror. A mirror indeed it was. In it was a picture of the shore with its fringe of cocoanut palms, with leaves waving like silvery feathers in the moonlight, with cadjan fisher huts with fires burning outside and women busy cooking the supper curries. Inka busiest of all.

"A pretty girl, to be sure," remarked his Majesty of the Ocean. "Pity her eyes are red with weeping. Never mind, Inka," he went on cheerily, so that the wavelets danced. "We'll look after Nanda."

Then came out the stepmother with her shrill voice shrieking "Inka?"

"Ya—rrh!" said the Ocean King in a voice like the bursting of a water-spout.

"The *Rakhsi!* Help! save me!" shrieked the terrified woman, again scuttling away as fast as she could go.

Now at the same time as all this was going on Nanda, the fisher lad, out in his *catamaran* on the ocean, was thinking of Inka, as indeed he always was. The sea was beautifully calm that night—never had Nanda seen it so calm; he was thinking as he prepared to cast his net. But just when about to throw his net, a picture arose from the very depths of that beautiful calm sea, a picture of Inka sorrowing, of the stepmother hiding the coral beads and the bangle in a hole of the mango tree, of the mango tree shaking and the stepmother in terror dropping the chattie, and Naga, old Naga the Cobra, coming and eating up the curry. Like a flash it passed before him. The scales fell from Nanda's eyes; Nanda no more could be deceived. Inka, his Inka, was true.

"Ho-ho?" said he, "I see! I see!"

Then something occurred. It sounded like the bursting of a thundercloud ; it *was* only the Ocean King's sneeze. Out of his element, his Majesty had caught cold.

"Ir-rush-rhr-yash!" sneezed he. At any rate it so turned the whole tide that Nanda and his *catamaran* were speedily brought to shore. In time, just in time to witness the Hare King bound back to his throne in the moon, old Naga the Cobra, not satisfied with the curry for supper, gobble up the wicked stepmother, and Inka awaiting her lover.

And all this was brought about by the Hare King's stroll that evening in the Paradise of Adam. Inka and Nanda were wed.

. . . . .

By this time they had arrived at the temple. Back from the road it stands—a Hindū temple of unknown date, one of the most ancient in Ceylon. Descending from the phaeton and entering the courtyard, whose stone pavement reeked with damp and mildew, the *Muttu*, being a Tamil of Southern India, was requisitioned as spokesman and interpreter to go and make known their desire to see and have an interview with the Brahman priest. The *Muttu* returned with the answer that the hour was passed—the sun had set.

Cynthia, who had had experience of other

monks in out-of-the-way monasteries in Europe said: "H'm! Go back, tell him an English Lady has come six thousand miles to see the learned *Brahman*. A disciple herself, she reveres learning, and trusts the *Brahman* of his wisdom may be pleased to see her."

The *Muttu* returned with the answer that as yet the last ray of the setting sun was still lingering on the land from the ocean, the *Brahman* would comply with the lady's gracious request.

In a minute or two he came out into the chill-striking courtyard where they awaited. A solemn stately *salaam* from a commanding figure of a man. A long white muslin scarf fell in graceful folds across his otherwise uncovered chest and down from his right shoulder to the waist, leaving his left shoulder bare. At the waist the scarf was wound round and round and confined, the same piece of muslin opened out doing duty as drapery for his lower limbs—yards and yards of muslin reaching to the sandals on his big brown feet. Withal an imposing figure, with a light on his broad intellectual brow. Those herculean shoulders might have marked the athlete, as the light on the brow denoted the thinker, the mystic, the dreamer. His dark eyes, downcast as became the monk, were raised once—a moment only. That moment sufficed to take stock, so to speak, of the European visitors. The Brahman spoke:

"Is the Lady anxious about anything?" he inquired in *Hindi.* "She appears so," he added. "Perhaps the Lady desires light, explanation, guidance, or advice? Something certainly has been troubling her of late."

Now Cynthia remembered something *had* been troubling her of late—something had been lost or stolen during their recent removal. One of the servants was the thief no doubt; but which, 'twas impossible to say. The loss and its attendant annoyance recurred to her now.

"If the Lady will give the date of her birth," continued the *Brahman,* "light may be forthcoming."

Cynthia complied by giving the date.

And now with a style on a huge *ola* leaf the *Brahman* traced a circle. This circle was then filled in with figures numerical, together with signs of the zodiac and of the planets, similar to a figure of the heavens cast for a horoscope. Presently:

"The Lady is born under Jupiter," said this Wise Man, the Hermit-Priest.

Cynthia recollected she had been told this before by a barrister friend in London who had "cast her nativity" when a girl of fifteen.

"Nobody can be ruined under Jupiter," continued the *Brahman.* "Enemies may try. The baleful rays of Saturn may cast shadows over the beneficent beams of Jupiter, darkening for a time; they will not prevail. The Lady," continuing after a brief space, "the Lady has been troubled in mind over a loss. An article is missing. The article is of greater length than breadth, and of two colours, with a patch of gay colours or a picture like a flower-bed. That article was stolen, the Lady will never see it again. The thief—a man with a scar on his left cheek—has taken it far away. It is in the possession of another man now—sold. Useless to trouble over it; it will never be restored."

In every particular the description of the article was correct. The personality of the thief Cynthia recognised as that of a man called in to assist the coolies in removing a heavy load, an incident she had entirely forgotten, although the man with the scar she remembered distinctly now. So *he* was the thief, and the servants were exonerated from blame. Cynthia heaved a sigh of relief.

Then, as the last glint of the sun's rays faded in the western horizon, the *Brahman* again *salaamed*, and, gathering his muslin drapings about him, departed into the sanctuary of the ancient temple.

CHAPTER XXIV

Mount Lavinia the Beautiful! — The advent of some of the ladies of the *Hárim* of Arábi Pacha—Cynthia decides to entertain *à la* London society lady — Husbands without their wives, it's easier: and nicer—Under the mangoes revelry — Lemon squash—Cynthia next day visits the ladies of the *Hárim*—Her embarrassment concerning a present —Must ask her husband—" Humph!"

MOUNT LAVINIA the Beautiful! Indebted indeed are the Europeans in Ceylon to your refreshing breezes from the wide, gleaming ocean!

Seated on the verandah of the palatial hotel—formerly the seaside residence of His Excellency —one realises not the fact of the equator's close proximity; one only realises a dream—a dream of nature's loveliness unsurpassed on this wonderful, beautiful earth.

"The Paradise of Adam," Cynthia was thinking as she sat alone, save for her companion Punch, in a shady, secluded corner where mosquitoes cease from troubling and the European is at rest. "The Paradise of Adam. What of Eve?"

Perhaps it was coincidence only that at that

moment a group of exceptionally strangely attired individuals—and one does see strange garbs in Ceylon—passed through the cocoanut wood down below. The courteous manageress coming that way just then, "Who are they?" asked Cynthia, waving her sunshade in that direction.

"The ladies of the *Hárim* of *Arábi Pacha* and party," was the reply.

"Indeed! How interesting!" Cynthia was up and looking after the group instanter—Punch likewise.

Coincidences are very curious, inexplicable except one has a knowledge of the stars and their courses, which, however, does not explain—it only signifies after all. That evening Cynthia's husband said, "I had an interview at the *Secretariat* to-day with some one who would interest you—*Arábi Pacha's* son. He tells me he has taken the bungalow down in the wood for: his wife, who is undergoing treatment for her eyes, and has to be near Colombo. He appears to be a very intelligent fellow. Shall I ask him up?"

"By all means. You know how interested I am in—people who *are* interesting. How much I should like to visit the ladies of a *hárim*, and see if all that the missionaries say about them is correct! We can't ask them to dinner; we don't know what they eat and what they don't eat——"

"They're *Mohammedans*, so they *may* not take their wives about with them," put in Cynthia's husband.

"Besides," said Cynthia, "we shouldn't know how many to allot to each. Well, let's do as the up-to-date society lady does, invite the men and leave out the wives. It's so easy to satisfy men —cigars, whisky and soda—oh! I'm forgetting again — they're not *Christians*. Well, say— lemon squash. We'll make the thing go, anyhow."

At five o'clock next evening the visitors came: Muhamed Ibn Ahmed Arábi Bey, eldest son of Arábi Pacha, and Ali Fehmy Pacha, a distinguished soldier, who for bravery had been rewarded with a wife of noble birth direct from the *Kedivial Hárim*, the Palace of Ismáil Pacha. Save for the fez, little was there in the dress and appearance of these two gentlemen to distinguish them from Europeans. *Gentlemen* they were in every respect. There was a plaintive note in the voice of Arábi Pacha's son, accentuated by the fact of his being totally blind in one eye. The brave Ali Fehmy Pacha took the tone of the major rather than minor, literally as well as metaphorically, as he had done doubtless throughout the campaign terminating in the battle of Tel-El-Kebir (July 1882), when Arábi, leader of the Egyptians in their revolt against injustice and oppression, had given up his sword to our General Lowe.

"Politics had best be avoided," Cynthia had said prior to the visit. "I'm desperately patriot when away from my native land." It was difficult, though, to keep to this decree—politics would "crop up," would enter into the conversation. With such fairness, such clemency these Egyptians spoke, however, that, as Cynthia said, "there was little fear of fighting Tel-El-Kebir over again under the mangoes in our compound." The visit passed pleasantly, amicably, instructively.

"Had the English but understood us and our purpose—our desires—your brave Lord Charles Beresford need not have bombarded our Alexandria. Personally we love as we admire the English, and are proud to say we have many friends among them," said Arábi Bey.

"And we trust madame will do our ladies the honour of calling upon them. My wife, Lady Aideel, will be delighted," added the Pacha Ali Fehmy.

"Indeed I will—to-morrow," said Cynthia. And she did.

At four o'clock next afternoon Cynthia wended her way to the bungalow in the cocoanut wood. To be straightforward, Cynthia had taken extra pains with her toilette and general personal appearance for this exceptional occasion. As she approached the verandah a couple of Sinhalese *ayahs* came forward as escort. "Lady coming, please, this way," said they, treading the stone steps that led to the verandah. Once there Cynthia was first apprised of Moslem seclusion. Instead of the verandah being open to light and air, except for the *tattie* sun screens as usual, *this* was draped and darkened. Nor were there the usual Singapore chairs and lounges—the ladies of the *hárim* were not wont to take their ease and the air on the verandah apparently. At the entrance to the bungalow, which was also curtained, contrary to the "customs of the country," a maid whose *khol*-blackened eyes shone out large and lustrous from the top of a *yashmak* came forward and took up the escort, the Sinhalese *ayahs* falling back. The room they entered was large and furnished *à l'Européen.* As a matter of fact the bungalow had been let to the Egyptians "furnished," and remained as it was, except for a few trifling additions such as photographs, flower-vases, &c., that evidenced feminine occupation with a certain refinement. Here, sinking into a Singapore chair, Cynthia, overcome with the fatigue and heat of walking, waited. A minute only, then—oh, was it possible? A tall, handsome, thoroughly European-looking lady in tailor-made skirt and white cambric blouse, entered, smiling and bowing and extending her hand. "Madame, this is kind of you to come to see us! I am the wife of Arábi Bey, and daughter (she meant daughter-in-law) of Arábi Pacha." Then her black eyes gleamed.

"But oh, madame! *comme vous être belle!* What a toilette! From Whiteley's—not? Ah, how *de*light-ful to see Whiteley's! One hears so much. And the figure—*pardon*, *madame*, may one ask how to keep the fat off? When the fat does arrive, *hélas!* our *marie* loves us no more! But how then, madame, to keep the fat off? *Comment?*"

Cynthia's eyes opened wide, very wide. Then she laughed.

"I thought," she said, "Mohammedans—*liked fat*. Christians always say so."

"Ah, madame, *mais ce n'est pas vrai. Pardon!* Madame is English—not? I then must *parler l'Anglais.* My *gouvernante* she was French. Such a pity—not? Ah! now comes Lady Aideen, and you have not told me of the fat, madame."

'Ere Cynthia had time to turn she found herself in the embrace of a giantess—a giantess garbed in voluminous robes of soft black Indian silk. When released, her discomposure not altogether abated on being held out at arms' length for inspection, while a torrent of French fell on her distracted hearing. Then, again, the embrace, kissing first on one cheek, then the other, then being held out at arms' length again. Cynthia felt faint. Not a breath of air seemed stirring in that much becurtained and bedarkened apartment. Cynthia well-nigh collapsed, while this effusive beauty of the *hárim* went on—all in French, with, however, occasional lapses into a language—perhaps Arabic—which was as Sanscrit to Cynthia. She *meant* well, though, this erstwhile captivating Circassian with the thick, long plait of brick-red hair falling down her broad, strong back, the Lady Aideen, wife of Ali Fehmi Pacha.

Compliments, eulogies were being showered on her, did Cynthia but know it. All she *did* know was it was intended as a kindly greeting, consequently was accepted as such, albeit it was overpowering—with the thermometer at over a hundred *Fahrenheit.*

"*Ma foi!*" Cynthia echoed that ejaculation when the Lady Aideen desisted, panting. The maid with the *yashmak* and *khol*-darkened orbs approaching at this juncture with a tray, afforded Cynthia and her hostesses a brief respite—a very brief respite.

"Tea, afternoon-tea, all English ladies like," observed Madame Arábi. "We like not tea: we take coffee. Madame will take sweetmeats?—cakes—not? And the fat, madame?"

"Thank you. Only a cup of tea," said Cynthia, proceeding to stir the tea; but the spoon stuck—stuck in a cup half full of sugar. Sweetened tea to Cynthia is poison—but that's a detail.

"Ahem! Are you ladies all Egyptians?" she asked now, when she had the chance of a word.

"Madame Aideen is Circassian, I Bedouin. My father was a Bedouin chief, and in my *jeunesse* we wandered—wandered far and always. Oh, it was a glorious life!"

"*Glorious*, it *must* have been!" echoed Cynthia.

"And, madame—does she love the Desert?—the great wide, glorious *Sahara?*"

Another surprise to Cynthia, who had been taught Mohammedan women were kept in a cage.

"Ah, but madame would love our Desert," continued the Bedouin, "—our glor-i-ous Sahara. Madame must come to Cairo some day—not?' And, rising, she caught Cynthia's hands in both her own, going off again into fresh rhapsodies over the "toilette of Monsieur White-ley."

"So you go back home sometimes?" said Cynthia, more interested in the Desert than in Westbourne Grove—far.

"Yes; your Government permits us to return, only our husbands not. *Hélas!* poor Father, he is old, and he longs for his native land! Yes, to us it is permitted. But oh! how the sea is terrible to us who have to stay down in our cabins, as you say, and never come up."

"Why not?" asked Cynthia.

A shriek from both ladies.

"*Mon enfant! les hommes!* They would see us—without veils! *Impossible!*"

"Well," said Cynthia, "it seems to me you take care to show the prettiest part of your faces—the brow and eyes. My husband saw you the other day——" Another double shriek.

"And—madame, what did your husband remark? He is very handsome, your husband—what did he remark of *us?*"

Cynthia told a fib. The ladies were delighted.

"But madame has no children?" Madame Arabi presently asked, after a brief but brisk dialogue in French, which seemed to Cynthia a jumble of toilettes and handsome husbands.

"No," said Cynthia, "I have not."

"*Pauvre madame!*" Again a bit of dialogue between the ladies; then Madame Arábi, spokeswoman, again said:

"Then madame shall have Zeinab. Ayah shall bring her now." Forthwith she clapped her little brown hands and gave the order for Zeinab to be brought. Zeinab appeared—a huge, fat baby in an *ayah's* arms.

"Here is Zeinab—fine, is she not? Fat for the baby is good—not? Zeinab is fine, fat.

Madame shall have her: we have others. Zeinab is for madame a present. To-day madame can take Zeinab away." This was followed on swiftly by instructions to the *ayah*, instructions for Zeinab's transfer and departure.

"I—I—" faltered Cynthia, "I—must ask my husband first. We *must* obey, you know. It is very, very kind of you, but—I *must* ask permission first," patting the fat cheek of the dark-eyed babe that eyed her knowingly, and, unlike Europeans of its age and experience, was disposed to permit of any familiarities without howling.

"*Mais oui, madame. C'est vrai!* That is true. We must obey When we come to see madame, then will Zeinab come too."

"Certainly. Certainly. Till then *adieu*," said Cynthia, rising.

"*Au revoir*, madame; not *adieu*. But, madame, the fat? Do not forget to tell. *Au revoir*." Again "*Au revoir*," when Cynthia was released from the second close embrace and could speak.

"Oh, no: I will not forget."

Cynthia drew a long breath when she emerged and found herself "in the open," where her husband awaited at a respectful distance in the Stanhope phaeton.

"You're going to receive a present—a baby," said she.

"Humph!" said he.

CHAPTER XXV

Their visit to the mountain capital — Kandy—The *Perehera* on—Everybody there—A splendid show The ugliest works of creation—Essentially Oriental : bizarre, picturesque—An imposing *tableau* as *finale* —" It almost reached the sublime."

IT was nearing the season when the great annual festival of the Sinhalese, called the *Perehera*, is held at Kandy, the mountain-capital. Accommodation had already been booked at the Queen's Hotel weeks before, as "everybody" is supposed to flock thither to witness the great show. The evening train from Colombo brought plenty of passengers, many of whom were awaited by the courteous manager of the Queen's with wagonettes and divers other vehicles. Cynthia was fascinated by the first glimpse of Kandy—a *bizarre* combination of the antique and the modern —civilisation and barbarism, in a setting of Nature's loveliest in landscape and in colouring. But the centre of interest is the Temple of the Tooth. At this season of the *Perehera* sleepy little Kandy wakes up. The little capital of the soft surrounding hills was a bee-hive of activity that evening of Cynthia's arrival. What a heterogeneous throng! Picturesque to a degree—even Europeans in their sun *topees* and *puggarees*, the ladies in white, lending to the picture, although few of them knew the meaning of the *Perehera*, or troubled themselves about it for that matter. They came—because it was "the thing" to come. The glow of sunset enhanced the colouring, endowing the scene with an unreality, a theatrical effect, which causes the newcomer to think it impossible to take life *au serieux* in Ceylon, particularly at holiday time. The invigorating air from the hills, moreover, has a champagne effect on one's system; one is conscious of exhilaration after the lowering influence of oppressive Colombo.

But the temple. *It* looms out stolidly: a memory in stone of ages, of histories, of people long bygone. Yes, stolidly it looms over the brilliant, bizarre scene—a memory, a memory in stone. It would be a huge effort of imagination to grasp all the subtle associations, sacred and secular, of that venerable pile, and say, the complex conveniences of the up-to-date Queen's Hotel at one and the same time. Cynthia was centuries behind the times when the wagonette drew up at the verandah.

"I have given you the best room, immediately overlooking the temple, whence the *Perehera* starts and returns," said the polite manager.

Photo. Plate, Ceylon

A GROUP OF SINHALESE MONKS IN THE PĀNSĀLA WITH PRIEST SEATED RECITING BANA

To be "the chiel amang 'em takin' notes" has its advantages sometimes.

After dinner a visit to the temple in the moonlight was decided upon. A mere "stone's-throw" from the hotel, even the European could so far exert himself or herself to go on foot.

Broad winding stone steps, always damp, mildewed, moss-grown, for the sun's rays never fall thereon, lead up to the towering temple—steps worn into hollows in the centre by the tramping of centuries upon centuries. At either end of each step was what Cynthia took for an effigy—a heathen god or goddess: it's always difficult to distinguish the sex of these deities—until, on tripping on her skirt, she stumbled against one of them, when—a yellowish-green eye was uplifted from the mask-like, putty face. *It* was a nun—one of a company from Burmah—Buddhist, of course.

Many Burmese *monks* they encountered later on—likewise here for the Sacred Festival. But although Cynthia decided they were the ugliest works of creation, *they* did appear *human*—the nuns did not.

The great distinction betwixt this temple and others of like age is the fact of its being the Shrine of Buddha's Tooth—the most sacred relic of Buddhism. Only on rare occasions and by special sanction is the Relic beholden.

To the infidel a hippopotamus's tooth would do as well. But the casket in which the Relic is preserved is a wonderful work of art and value combined—a casket of purest gold inlaid with magnificent gems. Taken altogether though, the effect is amazing rather than pleasing, the gems are too big and too numerous. Nevertheless the fineness of the filigree gold work is truly artistic and beautiful.

Inspection of this most famous temple completed, the *Perehera* was about to commence. No better place to witness the start than from that height. Although the moon made the night almost light as day, torches and lamps and lights of every description flared everywhere. As many human beings were clad in the skins of wild beasts of the jungle—tigers, leopards, cheetahs, monkeys, crocodiles, and buffaloes—it was difficult to define what was what, who was who. Elephants gorgeously howdahed and caparisoned lent dignity to the show: thirty-three elephants of the finest breed. On a level with the crimson and golden *howdahs*, mountebanks strode on stilts, whilst the "jungle creatures" kept up their profession by making night hideous with roaring, howling, chattering, shrieking.

A curious medley, in which the sublime and the ridiculous meet and merge, the former manifest in the companies of yellow-robed monks of ascetic gauntness, alms-bowl in one hand, palm-leaf in the other, the first to receive bounty of the charitable, the latter to ward off the glance of woman: "Look not on the face of woman lest thou be beguiled," said Siddharta the Buddha.

The procession was a mile in length, and took a couple of hours to complete the tour of the little town. Similar to the carnivals of Southern Europe, the *Perchera* has, though, a distinctive character of its own no *Western* nation can ever with impunity emulate: a distinction born of the East, the gorgeous, incongruous, grotesque, yet enchanting East. Three nights consecutively the *Perehera* is repeated; the fourth brings the completing ceremony, called the Dividing of the Waters. This ceremony is held on the banks of the river Mahavillagango at Peradeniya, a distance of some six miles from Kandy. Few Europeans attend this termination of the festival, as it is held at daybreak on the Friday. All the night previous people, animals, paraphernalia, the same motley crowd, likewise the holy element, the "faithful," in fuller force even than on the previous occasions, pilgrimage from all parts of Ceylon—aye, and from afar: India, Thibet, Burmah, and Japan—to be present at this sacred rite. The river is broad and clear here, and spanned by a handsome satinwood bridge. Amply rewarded did Cynthia consider herself for rising with the magpie (the lark of

Ceylon) on beholding that strangely fascinating assemblage congregating at the first faint streak of dawn on the bank of the Mahavillagango. As the hot sun rose, the gorgeous colours as seen through the morning mist were mellowed, as befitted the solemnity of the occasion. Priests and monks in yellow robes of every shade from saffron to cinnamon were there mixing with mountebanks and "monkies." The loud reverberation of a gun announced the commencement of the ceremony. A singular commingling of crude ideas of Hinduism with the gentler rites of Buddhism it appeared to Cynthia—fantastic, fascinating withal. Almost it seemed the "heavens" had opened and let loose other races, other beings, undreamt of in our human philosophy.

And towering above all was lordly Adam's Peak. Yes, and in the light of the dawning day the Footprint shone out—the first footprint of the first man, Adam, on his banishment to Lanka (Ceylon) in those first days of this world. At the given signal, the firing of the gun, a boat manned with monks bearing the Sacred Consecrated Thread put off from the crowded shore. As on the boat went plying the peaceful waters, *Bana* was recited by companies of priests on either side of the river —prayers and invocations. Once the river is crossed the Sacred Thread is secured on the opposite bank. Then a loud shout of triumph ascends, thrilling the early morning silence, vibrating the hills and echoing again and again.

The festival is over. The *Perehera* is completed. By that division of the water by the Sacred Thread evil is severed from good, dross separated from gold, purification has taken place, and thus they enter on another year.

As a *tableau* merely that scene on the beautiful river Mahavillagango in the pure and peaceful dawn could never be forgotten. It almost reached the sublime.

CHAPTER XXVI

Perideniya Botanical Gardens and a clairvoyante dream — A greeting from *Arábi Pacha* — Both Arábi and Cynthia are charmed—Cynthia learns to make "mocha" from the venerable Pacha—Funny little Nubians! — Arábi Pacha's piteous longing, "only to return home!"

IT was while here at the mountain capital that they availed themselves of making the acquaintance of *Arábi Pacha*, the Egyptian rebel, as he has been erroneously called by those not conversant with his purpose and his aim. As head of the War Department of his native land, *Arábi*, possessed of a personality born to attract and to lead, had been chosen as the defender of justice and the rights of his people—a man of "singularly uncommon honesty," as Lord Charles Beresford, his adversary in the campaign of 1882, honourably designated him. But this is no political treatise. All 'tis necessary to say is that *Arábi Pacha*, having capitulated, was then an exile, a British captive in Ceylon. It had been arranged that Cynthia and her husband should drive in the early morning to Perideniya, to visit the Botanical Gardens there, prior to making a call on *Arábi Pacha*, who, with some of his family, was at that time residing in a comfortable bungalow situated at top of a hill midway between Kandy and Perideniya. Soon after daybreak, accordingly, they started in a victoria. The mountain air was fresh and invigorating, although once the sun is up the mountain capital soon becomes hot almost as Colombo, until the tropical sun goes down. Tickets to enter the gardens had been taken; all they had to do was to enjoy that delightful drive in the freshness of the morn.

Few people were about; those few, however—natives going to or returning from their bath—contributed to the picturesque scenery. It is marvellous the grace with which a native's drapery falls in folds. Careless, unpremeditated; no sculpture could manifest more perfect artistic effect. The gorgeous colours, moreover, blend, always harmoniously, no matter how vivid, while the gait of the Oriental is dignity with ease combined.

Cynthia, accustomed as she was to driving through one of the loveliest portions of Europe—Southern Austria—experienced a new sensation now: the spell, the fascination of the East, incomparable to any other as it is indescribable. Silently they drove along, the giant trees casting a pleasant shade, until on turning a corner Cynthia started.

"Ah!" rising to her feet in the carriage.

"What place is this? I know it well; I have surely been here before!" she exclaimed, excitedly.

"The entrance to the Botanical Gardens. We get out here," was her husband's reply.

"The—entrance—to—the—Botanical—Gardens," repeated Cynthia alighting, yet keeping her regards fixed on those iron gates, with the ticket-taker's shed just within, at an angle of the road. "No, I have *not* been here before. And yet it is all so familiar. It was a dream I had, repeated again and again in my early girlhood. Now that dream that haunted my youth is realised. *Every detail I have beheld before.* All is familiar to me. I will show you where the paths lead. Come."

They entered, giving up their tickets at the shed, and Cynthia trod those magnificent gardens, leading the way as though it were familiar to her—as indeed *it was—in dream.*

Let psychical research explain this. Cynthia relates the fact only, at the same time recalling those lines of Rossetti:

> *I have been here before,*
> *But when or how I cannot tell:*
> *I know the grass beyond the door,*
> *The sweet, keen smell,*
> *The sighing sound, the lights around the shore.*

* * * * *

Arábi Bey, or, to give him his full name, *Muhamed Ibn Ahmed*, *Arábi Pacha's* eldest son, was to meet them at his father's house. As up they mounted to the bungalow by the zigzag foot-path hedged with roses—glorious roses from seeds of trees grown on the Bosphorus, roses large as a saucer, and laden with perfume that scented the air within a radius of, say, half a mile—as up they mounted *Arábi Bey* descended to meet them.

"My father is charmed to make your acquaintance," said he, shaking hands with the visitors.

Upon entering the bungalow a commanding figure dressed *à l'Européen*, except for a fez, rose and bowed low. Then a hand was uplifted in military salute.

"How do you do? We are so pleased to come to see you. I hope you are well?" said Cynthia, coming forward and offering her hand.

The grave, sad countenance relaxed in a smile. "May I sit here—beside you?"

The smile expanded. Cynthia—that strange "writing woman," friend of Princes, Peasants, Prisoners of War—everybody, but—snobs, shams, and sycophants—took her seat on a cane chair beside *Arábi Pacha* on his prayer-carpet on a *divan*.

What impressed Cynthia most in this her first

interview with *Arábi* the Exile was his Faith in Providence, the Almighty.

"What the Almighty decrees comes to pass," said he, quoting the *Korán.* "What He desires not happens not. All power is with Him."

It was impressive, to say the least of it, to hear with what clemency, what resignation, and with what *unshaken faith* this defeated warrior spoke of his defeat. The *Korán*, ever by his side, had been his guide, was still his guide, would always be his guide.

"Remain constant in Faith, and you will merit commendation and gain eternal repose," was now as it ever had been his text. And unlike some others, *not* of Moslem Faith, he acted on and up to it.

"I felt in my heart our fate—the fate of all Egyptians—was in the hands of England," he said. "It was for England to continue and to complete the work the Almighty had decreed I should begin—*and England will*," he added.

But the fragrant aroma of coffee caused the conversation to take a different turn—real Mocha.

"What delicious coffee!" exclaimed Cynthia, to give the conversation a turn. *Arábi Pacha* smiled.

"Now," went on the old man, quite cheerfully, "I will teach you to make coffee as we do. Then tell me how you like it." Forthwith he commenced handling the brass utensils on the tray brought in by an ebony-black Nubian, grinning from ear to ear. Excellent coffee it was. Cynthia had three cups, to *Arábi's* apparent delight. Then, in the midst of lively social chat, in which *Arábi Bey* (the eldest son) and his brother—a remarkably fine, handsome young man—joined, the curtains were drawn, and in scampered three or four chocolate-coloured youngsters with close-cropped hair on shining pates. What little hair there was was "laid out in paths," so to speak, tiny, close-cut ringlets in rows across the head—a most peculiar effect. Their faces, although far from prepossessing, were full of animation, and just now expressive of great joy. Rushing up to the commanding figure on the divan, they threw their naked brown arms around his neck, pressed their flat noses against his cheek, and literally smothered him with caresses, chattering volubly all the while. *Arábi*, the leader, the commander of men, accepted these ebullitions of affection in the spirit of the intention. He bore those caresses with the spirit of happy resignation. Indeed, this big, brave warrior allowed those little half-castes to do what they liked with him. Then, giving them sugar and sweetmeats, they turned their attention elsewhere, scampering round the visitors "like cannibals around a fat missionary."

"What funny little creatures! Who are

they?" asked Cynthia, throwing them lumps of sugar.

"My brothers and sisters," was *Arábi Bey's* reply.

* * * * *

*Ahmed Arábi, the Egyptian.**

One of the many gracious and kindly actions of His Majesty King Edward on accession to the throne was to cancel the captivity of *Arábi Pacha* and his brother exiles, and permit them to return home.

* Arabic autograph in Cynthia's birthday-book.

CHAPTER XXVII

Cynthia's preference for the handsome Afghan—An officer's story in response—"*Allah is great! Allah is good!*"—A Moslem's inflexible faith.

"OF all the different nationalities I've seen in Ceylon I like the Afghan best," said Cynthia one day to a friend, an Officer in the ——shire Regiment, at that time stationed in Colombo.

"You don't know them as I do," was the reply. "Although there are decent chaps among them—real religious, too, their *faith's* simply marvellous—I don't allude to their gymnastics on "prayer-carpets" before the rising and setting sun, I mean their *solid belief*, don't you know—it's marvellous! A chap in the ——shire told me a story about one—a *true* story. I'll tell it you, if you like; but mind, I'm not much good at story-telling."

"Well," said he, in answer to Cynthia's "Do—do," "here goes," flicking the end off his cigar, and refreshing his memory with whisky and soda. But as the narration was somewhat discursive, Cynthia, making mental notes, put it into more regular form afterwards. Here is the story.

Mahmoud, the Afghan

"An earthly paradise were it not for the insects."

"And the snakes, Mrs. Seymour," put in the Captain, drawing up a lounger to the side of his Colonel's wife, an Englishwoman pretty still and young looking, notwithstanding the anæmic look one gets after a year or two's residence in tropical Ceylon.

"And the snakes, certainly. You haven't forgotten my affinity—and aversion combined, Captain? Affinity, for were there a snake in a whole *Korale*, as they say here, it would give the preference to me," said Mrs. Seymour ruefully, fanning herself.

"'Not like to like but like in difference,' as Tennyson would say." Captain O'Ryan was a thorough-bred Irishman, and the most popular man in the Regiment—with the ladies; a bachelor too. A striking contrast to his Colonel, who, a typical Englishman, was slow of tongue though sure, and deficient in those subtle turns of speech merely suggestive of compliment, dear to the fair sex.

"No: it's downright affinity, it *must* be, or I wouldn't attract them as I do."

Mrs. Seymour had had a dinner party that evening and the guests were now assembled on the spacious verandah of the Colonel's fine bungalow facing the Officers' Mess House in Colombo: coffee and liqueurs being handed round by native *Appoos* in immaculate white.

"Sure and you hypnotise them, thin," retorted the Captain, affecting the softest brogue and throwing expression into his lustrous Irish eyes.

Mrs. Seymour shrugged her white shoulders—having been pretty and attractive to the opposite sex all her life compliments came to her lightly—and went. "How hot it is!" she said. "No coffee; bring me an iced lemon squash," to a servant.

"Mrs. Seymour, we must have your opinion. The Afghan's come with the things—lovely! Do come!"

A young girl had left a group at the other end of the verandah, and with an arch glance at the Captain, addressed the hostess.

"Come, has he?" Languidly Mrs. Seymour rested her hand on the arm of her Singapore chair and was about to rise when she was conscious of feeling something soft and clammy cold beneath two or three fingers of that hand. She withdrew it hastily and uttered a cry. Captain O'Ryan ceased speaking to Miss D'almaine and turned his regards just in time to see a long black snake, or the latter portion of one, glide away in the dark shade of the palms and plants.

"A snake! I touched its head—ur-rh!" Mrs. Seymour shuddered. "Why, *why* do they always come to me? Ur-rh! how I loathe them!"

"Lady not killing cobra, cobra bringing lady good luck," said an *Appoo,* who himself would have been terrified out of his life at such perilous proximity: natives are awful cowards, particularly the Sinhalese.

"Come, dear Mrs. Seymour, and look at these embroidered muslins, they're *too* lovely; just the things for the *tableaux.* Never mind the cobra, it's gone; and cobras *do* bring good luck" (with another glance at the Captain) "a clairvoyante in London told me so," said Meta D'almaine.

The Colonel had now come up, observing the commotion, and drawing his wife's hand through his arm, said "Don't be alarmed. It wasn't a cobra: only a rat-snake, from what I saw of it. It wouldn't harm you."

Mrs. Seymour sighed, but it was a sigh of relief: she always felt safe when her husband was near. The Colonel carried an atmosphere of protection and security about with him. Women felt this and liked and respected him for it, albeit he awed them. Many, too many, prefer a fool who can flirt.

"Only a rat-snake? A rummy sort of rat-snake then." It was a lieutenant who talked—he always did. "Didn't you see that glittering

ring round its body? *I* did. By George! I never saw one like it."

Every one laughed: some one said, "Your geese are all swans, Hardy. "Some one else said, "Fireflies;" some one else suggested "glow-worms," "radium," and so forth.

"All the same I saw it," maintained the young lieutenant, who, undaunted by the banter, launched forth one of his own special and remarkable stories for the edification of any who would listen to it.

Meanwhile a group surrounded a man of swarthy complexion in very picturesque costume of white nainsook with elaborately embroidered zouave in red velvet and gold, a *cummerbund* of crimson silk in which were carried poignards and pistols, sandals and turban, the latter with the conical centre marking the nationality and religion of *Mahmoud the Afghan*, itinerant vendor of Oriental silks, stuffs and embroideries. Calmly, with a certain *hauteur*, he stood looking on while his *coolie* opened out the goods for inspection. The men of the party after a remark or two strolled away, leaving the ladies to make their purchases.

Mahmoud the Afghan was a man of few words. He stood there, silent, except when asked a question—the price usually—by one of the ladies, stood with a calmness, a dignity almost amounting to disdain, or, as Meta D'almaine averred, "like Byron's *Lara*."

"My things all good, Lady. I ask one price—cheap price, for all good things, Lady." Then he would state the price, but was content, perfectly content, to accept one-half. Ultimately the purchases were completed. The ladies were delighted with their "bargains." The Afghan commanded the coolie to cord the bundles, then with a grave *salaam* retired.

Suddenly, "Where is my bangle? Gone!" exclaimed Mrs. Seymour. Immediately skirts were drawn aside, frills and furbelows shaken. Not a trace of the bangle was there.

"I was wearing it, I know. *You* remember, Captain O'Ryan, when I was talking to you on that chair, I was twirling it. You *must* remember." Mrs. Seymour spoke vehemently. She was in such earnest. She prized that bangle more than any article she possessed.

The Captain *did* remember. "To be sure," said he, "I noticed it when— " he was going to say "the snake appeared," but with true Hibernian tact substituted, "when you rose to go to the Afghan."

The Afghan! Ah!

"My bangle! my beloved bangle! my betrothal gift! I would not have lost it for worlds."

"Lost *what?*" The Colonel had been inside

the bungalow with three others at whist, so had to be told.

"Never mind, Lucy," said he, with a tender strain in his usually stern voice. "There are other bangles to be bought. Don't distress yourself, dear."

Men can't comprehend the element of sentiment attached to inanimate things as women do. To himself he was saying, "That d—d Afghan!" The same thought was in every mind: the adjective only varying and adapting itself to the individual or the sex.

Meta D'almaine, said "that *awful* Afghan!" Where was her "Lara" now?

"Rogues, every one of 'em, these natives," was the unanimous decree. Mrs. Seymour of course had dropped the bangle whilst handling the goods; the Afghan had detected it, and with Oriental agility, which is nothing short of *legerdemain*, had secreted and secured it.

Of course! There could be no two opinions about it.

The Colonel should take out a summons against Mahmoud the Afghan next day.

Next day Colonel Seymour did.

II

The Colombo Police Court was packed with people, people of every nationality under the sun it seemed, for in complexion they ranged from chocolate brown to the waxen fairness of the Anglo-Saxon. Conspicuous among them was the tall and imposing figure of an Afghan, defendant in the action now about to be heard. His *khol*-blackened eyes had in them a wistful, far-away look as of one half dazed, half above and beyond things terrestrial, the gaze of a seer or a dreamer. His raiment, spotlessly clean, was set off by an elaborately embroidered *zouave* beneath which daggers, poignards and pistols, handsomely wrought, gleamed in the crimson silk *cummerbund.* His turban, one of those with the conical centre which nearly was the cause of a second Mutiny owing to the want of tact of some Europeans in adapting the same for the headgear of their horse-keepers—his turban distinctive of his caste, religion and nationality, sat gracefully as well as jauntily on his flowing raven locks. A picturesque figure of a man was he. All eyes turned instinctively, centred and fixed themselves on him—Mahmoud the Afghan, the accused. Mahmoud the Afghan met them unmoved.

Several European ladies were in Court—a very exceptional thing in Ceylon, where gossip and indolence make up the average European woman's existence. Many were here to-day, however, and still many more were the remarks of admiration passed from their æsthetic point of view. "*What* a fine man! Who would say he was such a thief? Quite hard to believe, isn't it now?"

"Confounded rascals and thieves all of them," being the answer of the stronger sex.

"You can't judge from appearances, Mrs. Seymour, especially these Orientals. They may 'look like gods,' as you women put it, they *act* like —ahem! all the same. These Afghans, too, have a habit of lopping you off without the slightest rhyme or reason, much less provocation. Homicidal mania it's called—comes over them at times, they *must* murder their best friend if nobody else is in the way. I knew a man——"

But the Lieutenant's forthcoming story, an interesting one no doubt, was "kilt intirely," as the Irishman would say, by the opening of the Court.

The first witness called was Mrs. Seymour, the owner of the missing or stolen article, a gold bangle set with emeralds and diamonds, valued at £150 sterling. Mrs. Seymour having been sworn, gave her evidence in a calm, yet gentle manner, not apparently altogether unreluctantly. Truth to tell, much as she prized the bangle, and mourned its loss, she would rather her husband had not taken out the summons. But Lucy Seymour was not a suffragette; indeed she was old-fashioned in some ways, one of them being content to bow to her husband's decision. Men seem to think only the *plain* wives, the "homely" ones as the Americans call them, do this, but there, my lords of creation, you are mistaken, as you are in imagining those unattractive ones are more amiable: A plain woman has a grudge against the whole world, and takes it out in spite, and other little mean ways.

But pretty Mrs. Seymour was answering the Magistrate's questions—a young Scotsman as much conversant with law as the quill he wielded. Every instant, though, her regards wandered in the direction of the accused. Those wistful eyes seemed to draw them. Within them there appeared to be hidden volumes. She was thinking if only she might look long and steadily enough into that placid and profound countenance she would be told the truth, the mystery would be revealed. "Mystery, pshaw!" said some one when she called it such. Yes, more than ever as she stood in the witness-box now she had this feeling upon her. Those eyes were veritable wells. Truth was at the bottom. How to reach it? This, the question she was asking herself; the question she knew not how to answer.

Meanwhile the Magistrate's queries came in quick succession. All the witness had to do was answer "Yes" or "No." When she would elaborate she was interrupted. This is law: law is not always justice.

When Mrs. Seymour left the witness-box and was met by her husband, she looked pale, very pale. The Colonel half regretted having taken the action. The ordeal was too much for the wife whom he loved. He led her to the carriage, and sent for a glass of port wine.

"Julian, I *know* that man is innocent," she said when she had revived a bit.

"Go home, dear—and rest," and stooping so that no one should see, the Colonel kissed his wife: Englishmen would rather face a volley than be seen kissing. Captain O'Ryan gave evidence to having seen the bangle on Mrs. Seymour's arm up to the time when she rose to go to the Afghan. All the other guests at the dinner party were there to testify to having seen it worn that evening, if need be. Circumstantial evidence all of it; nevertheless pointing directly at the Afghan. Who else could have stolen it? Where else could it be? The mind of every European present—now that Mrs. Seymour had left on the plea of not feeling well—the mind of *every* European present, the Magistrate included, was made up, as a matter of fact had been made up before the first witness had entered the box. The bangle had fallen from Mrs. Seymour's arm, been picked up by the Afghan, and dexterously secreted and purloined. What more simple? What more natural—to an

Oriental? Clear as noonday. It needed but to be related to convict him. But law demands a little more than that, even in our First Crown Colony. It must be proven. This was the difficulty.

All the man Mahmoud had to say in defence was a denial, absolute denial of ever having *seen* the bangle. And in his deep dark eyes there was no shifting, no prevarication, only calm steady persistency in denial. The Magistrate was, as a matter of fact, a little nonplussed. He occupied himself energetically in scribbling. Meanwhile, an undertone colloquy was going on among a little group of sallow and olive-skinned men in strange garb, made up of East and West, a compromise betwixt the two. The outcome of the confab was a paper handed up to the Magistrate, who, speaking to a man at his elbow, nodded assent in answer. Then the Clerk of the Court rising said it was his duty to state that numerous letters testifying to the good character—*exceptionally* good character—of the accused had been sent in —letters from merchants of good standing who declared they had known the man and had had dealings with him for years. All bore testimony to his honesty.

The face of every European present wore a smile: Many said "*H'm.*" And all this while the hands of the clock moved round. The tropical sun streamed in hotter and hotter. The gun from the fort boomed 4 o'clock. The Court rose, the case against Mahmoud the Afghan was adjourned, "to come on again on the 19th—ten days' time." The European ladies looked whiter than ever when they took their seats in their phaeton, dog-cart or buggy. They had had their novel experience of a Police Court—"in the Tropics, too, my dear," as they afterwards proudly explained, but—they didn't want it repeated. "Poor dear Mrs. Seymour, the heat was too much for her. She doesn't want him convicted either! I'm sure of it. She'd rather lose her bangle, though it *was* a love gift from the Colonel. Well, he is a handsome fellow—that Afghan, I mean. I wonder how he gets up his eyes like that? I wish I knew. The secret would be a fortune to Mme. Xerxes of Bond Street. Heigho! how much do you think he'll get, Captain? What a boon to have something fresh to talk about! We were all getting so frightfully *blasé*."

Yes, it was indeed a boon to have "something fresh to talk about." It was the talk of the Mess, of the Club, of the Tennis Racquet and Golf Links, of the Drive, and of King's House—*the* talk. The ladies even developed a little colour in their lips and cheeks over it, *natural* colour. The men had bets on, of course. Every one seemed to wake up over it and enjoy it—every one save Mrs.

Seymour. She was silent and apparently rather sad. "But then—poor dear!" vaguely remarked her "best friend." And the Colonel—but he was never a man of many words. Only a shrug of their white shoulders was bestowed on him.

III

It was Lucy Seymour's custom to be in the saddle before daybreak, when the air even of Colombo is fresh and invigorating. When the sun comes up with its rapidly increasing heat outdoor exercise for Europeans is practically impossible. Escorted by the Colonel, when his duties permitted, otherwise attended by a horse-keeper, for their establishment did not include an English groom, a *Muttu*, who took short cuts on foot to meet his *Durasani* at intervals, she would ride out to Mount Lavinia by the road, returning by the sea-shore. Delightful indeed was the sea-breeze as over the damp sand she cantered, the mare a high-mettled Waler enjoying it as much as her mistress. Lucy Seymour's mind was an active one naturally, action rendered it more so. When troubled or perplexed about anything she sought solution or relief in her "mount."

"It sets the mental machinery agoing and in order," she would say to her husband. "I'm never so bright as when in the saddle. The cobwebs disperse and one sees and understands ever so much clearer. But I *must* get away from people—acquaintances I mean."

This was why the Colonel's wife so far transgressed the decrees of Mrs. Grundy, presiding Genius of the European Community of Ceylon, as to have a will and a way of her own—and exercise both. Sometimes she would ride out far amongst the outlying villages in the moonlight. Thus it was she came to see and know more about the people—the natives, who, at first resenting because of their innate prejudice to horse-womanship, came soon to look out for the "*Mahatmaya*-Officer's Lady," and welcome her winsome face with smiles. The Colonel demurred at first, but never was he so proud of his wife as when in the saddle. He had every confidence in her ability as a horse-woman, and notwithstanding her pretty face—"doll's face," some called it—she was plucky. Only when her finer feelings were hurt Lucy Seymour gave in. This particular morning she was feeling very perplexed. The three days which had elapsed since that Police Court affair had been anxious, troubled ones. Instead of allaying that feeling—that curious inexplicable feeling amounting to assurance concerning the Afghan's innocence, the days and hours only augmented it. What should she do to prove it?

What *could* she do? She was thinking now as her mare ambled along the red road leading to beautiful Mount Lavinia. "He's not guilty: he's not guilty," seemed to be the refrain of the springy action of the Australian bred. The twice or thrice she had said this to her husband a shade had passed over his brow and on the last occasion his tone in answer had been nearer anger than any ever addressed to her before. "Lucy, have you no more sense than to let your kindly heart override your judgment? Dismiss it from your mind if it distresses you," he had said.

Ah! Colonel, if we poor human creatures could but act up to your stalwart advice!

Lucy Seymour had *not* dismissed it from her mind. It haunted her. Spite of her immense respect as well as love for her husband she could not obey him in this, nor become convinced. *The Afghan was not guilty. She knew it.* Somehow she came to associate the solution of the mystery with her morning ride: how or why she knew not. Soon as she awoke the thought, the anxiety was with her. Some power or intelligence seemed to urge her to the fulfilment of something she alone could accomplish—some act of justice. Sometimes on her homeward canter along the beach it was as though a voice spoke not in her ears, but from *within*, "Prove it: spare him," it seemed to say. This she kept to herself. The "world" might have decreed her insane, the "world" being so very wise himself, particularly so—"his wife"

But though the conviction gripped her like a hypnotic suggestion she knew not how to proceed, how to devise a way or means whereby to work her conviction into proof. "How weak we women are, after all! If only Julian saw and understood as I do!" she said again to herself while passing *Bambalapitiya*. Then she sighed. "Why *are* we so weak?"

"Dear Mrs. Seymour, did you notice his eyes? full of magnetism. I'm sure he's a hypnotist," Meta D'almaine had said. Then Lieutenant Hardy had capped her remark with one of his stories—a blood-curdler based on Oriental Black Art and hypnotism.

"Was it a fact?" Mrs. Seymour had asked herself more than once. She was sensitive—"*a* sensitive," according to the Society for Psychical Research. Had he hypnotised her—that day in court? She had turned very faint after giving evidence, and felt miserable—miserable ever since. Had the Afghan hypnotised her? Orientals are adepts in the Art, by study, education, heredity. Certainly the thought, the conviction of this man's innocence possessed her, like an obsession. Day and night it never left her. When she dreamed it was there in some guise or another, increasing, strengthening, until this morning it seemed to have reached a crisis. *The Afghan was innocent.* It was for her to prove it. And with this thought filling her mind she put the mare into a canter with a brush of the switch, fully determined to carry this conviction out. *How?* She no longer asked herself that! She was going to do it. That sufficed.

When she turned in at the gateway of the bungalow the Colonel awaited her on the verandah.

"Come, Lucy," he said kindly, as he took her hand to dismount. "You stay out too long. You fatigue yourself. The sun is well up besides. You're looking pale. Come and have tea."

Running his eyes over the Singapore chairs, the Colonel selected the most comfortable for his wife, who sank into it with a sigh of relief, then looked up into the face of the commanding figure of her husband with a light in her eyes—the light of deep affection that lasts when passion's fire is long burnt out. "Thank you, Julian dearest. I wish every woman had such a husband—how different the world would be!"

The Colonel laughed and pulled Lucy's ear—a pretty shell-like ear. He couldn't pay a compliment if his life depended on it. He *could* storm a fortress though, and be firm and steadfast as the Rock of Gibraltar in his devotion to one woman—which is rarer still.

Chota Hazira on the verandah, ere yet the day is spoilt by the heat, dust and glare, is delightful in Ceylon. Lucy drank her tea and ate the *appas* and felt ever so well—and happy. It seemed a great load was slipping from her heart. Her husband's keen blue eye detected colour coming into her lips and cheeks. He would have liked to say something about "the roses," but didn't know how. He felt such a "bull in a china shop" if he ventured on anything of the sort. Lucy often chaffed him on the way he proposed: He liked her chaff—his steely eyes twinkled over it: She was chaffing him now: She always did when she felt light-hearted. Suddenly, she knew not why, she was feeling light-hearted now. For the first time since the loss of the bangle she felt light-hearted.

"Half-past eight!" she exclaimed, "and I ordered my bath at eight." Clapping her hands, an *Appoo* appeared. "Tell *Ayah* I'm ready for the bath, and take these things away."

"All right, Lady."

"Don't say all right, Lady, say Yes, Ma'am. It's more polite—correct I mean. He's in the raw, Julian, but he'll make a good servant. These natives are like dough, one needs a light yet firm hand to mould them. He's a treasure—in embryo.

"*Another* treasure, Lucy?" The Colonel was chaffing now.

"Didymus!" was the reply, standing on her tiptoes to kiss the curly moustache.

"I'm off." And with a song on her lips away Lucy Seymour went to the dressing-room to prepare for her bath.

"Strange creature of moods am I!" she was thinking as she commenced to take off her riding habit. "Only an hour ago—less, I had that awful load on my breast, that still more awful anxiety teasing my mind. *Now* I—oh! how happy I am! What a beautiful world we're living in! That dear, glorious sun, how it glorifies the Lake! What a picture for an artist! No (to the *Ayah*) don't shut out that lovely view; leave the *jalousie* half turned —so. More than ever I'm in love with the view this morning!"

"*Durasani* feeling happy more this morning. *Durasani* looking sad, very, some days. Not now more. Liver good, no?"

"You're right, *Ayah*. I suppose it *was* liver." The *liver* is the pivot on which the whole mechanism of existence turns and depends according to the European's point of view in the East.

"Great joy p'raps coming to *Durasani*. Lizard always coming out speaking: *Durasani* not hearing, seeing? *I* see, *Appoo* see, *Muttu* see."

"That little lizard there? Oh yes, he came and clucked at me soon as I got up this morning. So he is the harbinger of good luck, eh? Well, let's hope so. And now take these things and hang them in the sun. Give me the bath towels. That's all. You may go now, Ayah."

Mrs. Seymour had another peep through the *jalousie*. That view of the Colombo Lake always charmed her. This morning it looked lovelier than ever. It was the season of blossom. The trees were laden with them; conspicuous the *flambeau* with its wide-stretching branches dependent with flame-coloured bells several feet in length. Then the feathery tamarisk and the filigree bamboos glinting in the sunlight, while majestic palms towered aloft, waving their graceful golden plumes. And below lay the water of the Lake, a sheet of burnished gold.

Lucy Seymour sighed. "It's too lovely!" she said, as she turned away. For a moment she felt sad. People of fine sensibilities are always affected so by the beauties of nature. Then the joy of life came over her again, and singing as she went, she wended her way to the bath-room. No sooner was the door opened than the song died on her lips. Lucy Seymour stood transfixed. It was as though a sudden blow on the head had opened an inner vision. It was not fear that made her stand there speechless: It was not horror that transfixed her. Indeed her feeling was one of intense joy. And yet—within a yard or two of her sandalled feet there was her natural antipathy. A snake—a huge black rat-snake—but now wriggled from under the bath, which stood on cement blocks, and now confronted her with head erect, and almost on a level with her own. Strangest of all, some foot or more down its wriggling neck it wore a band of jewels, which catching the sunrays coming in through the *jalousies* glinted and glistened in her very eyes.

For fully a couple of minutes Lucy Seymour stood thus: the snake equally as astonished apparently: each looking into the other's eyes. Not a vestige of fear possessed her. Her silence was due to sheer amazement. She was speechless. But suddenly a sense of the *reality* of the situation occurred to her. Her one thought then was her husband. "Julian! Julian!" she called. That seemed to break the spell. While silence reigned the snake had kept its steady gaze upon her. Now down went its head, its body wriggling away in the direction whence it had come, making for the water sluice. But, for some reason —the bath being unevenly poised probably, the ormament encircling its sinuous body impeded it. Desperate endeavours the snake made, but failed.

The Colonel came immediately in response to

his wife's call. Immediately, too, he saw the snake—*wearing the late missing bangle.* That was a detail, however, in his anxiety for his wife. She was snatched up in his strong arms and borne to a lounger on the verandah before she could utter. Then "Go, Julian," she said.

The Colonel knew what she meant. He only waited an instant to assure himself Lucy was all right. "Look after the *Durasani, Ayah,*" said he. "Boy! bring me a revolver—quick."

Natives glory in fire-arms and sport of any kind. Half a minute later a report was heard through the Colonel's bungalow and across the Lake: And within another thirty seconds the lost bangle was in the owner's lap.

"Oh, Julian, how happy I am to have it back!" Perhaps some wives would have said, "I told you so." Lucy Seymour did not. The Colonel pressed her hand. His countenance though glad was grave. His wife's intuition told her why.

* * * * *

When Mahmoud the Afghan had the news of his release brought to him in the House of Detention he was at prayer, kneeling on his prayer-carpet facing his Mecca—for it was eventide. No notice did he take whatever of the announcement until three times he had made his obeisance and his prayer was finished. Then, when he realised he was a free man—unsuspected, his character unstained, again he turned his *kohl*-darkened eyes in that direction—the shrine of his faith, and muttered "Allah is Great! Allah is Good!" and gathering his prayer-carpet and few other belongings together, passed out of the iron gate as the last bright rim of the golden sun sank deep into the Indian Ocean.

Mahmoud is now the leading merchant in Kabul. How this came about Colonel Seymour best could tell. But he doesn't. English-like he is too reserved.

CHAPTER XXVIII

The fascination of the East: what it is, and what it isn't — Cynthia's new venture — A *podyan* (page boy) from India—Friday's advent—Friday's progress—Friday's escapade, and its result—A small chapter of "customs of the country."

IF one is asked what is the fascination of the East, it is difficult to reply: but that there *is* a fascination it would be useless to deny. The atmosphere is charged with it. The European may pass a restless night on pillows and mattress wet through with perspiration, and bitten unmercifully by a stray mosquito slipped in under the net curtains, nevertheless as soon as one looks out on the sun-lit landscape, with the natives loitering along with their picturesque grace, one is caught by the spell. No matter the worries, the annoyances—Cook drunk and incapable of cooking the dinner when you return ravenously hungry from your long moonlight ride or drive, and in no country is appetite more keen or compulsory in its demands—nature *must* be aided by frequent sustenance in this enervating climate; no matter how often upon taking one's seat at table the mustard spoon, the butter-knife, the sugar-tongs, or what not is missed never to return again—every day it's something, from one's umbrella to a tea-pot—in spite of the mosquitoes attacking one's eyelids, ears and feet, morn noon and night; ants of six varieties and degrees of ferocity devouring the Indian matting, the sugar, the vitals of the piano, and one's own human substance, silver fish ruining one's linen and laces, and causing havoc amongst one's books; scorpions that have a predilection for one's bed; cockroaches, centipedes, locusts, tarantulas, and myriads of other pests, including snakes that haunt the bath, and spiders whose web is as strong as a thread of silk: notwithstanding the fact that everything edible must stand in a vessel of water on account of the invading insects, and even then, although the four legs of the dining-table are thus fortified, no sooner is the cloth laid than regiments of ants parade and lay siege to anything placed thereon ere the *Appoo* has time to turn and with the crumb-brush disperse the enemy: notwithstanding the mildew, which in a few hours converts one's black leather shoes into green, and causes everything from picture frames to books to fall to pieces: not to mention the daily scenes and tragedies with and amongst the native servants which go on even in the best-regulated households; nor to omit the inevitable fact of one's declining health and strength, nevertheless there remains the charm, the fascination that, once experienced, can never be shaken off, resisted nor forgotten.

To attempt to graft European habits and principles on to the Oriental, however, is waste of time and energy. Cynthia tried it. Given the *raw* material—that is fresh, uncorrupted—by the power of influence, early instruction and environment, she argued, much might be achieved. With this end in view she sent to India for a small boy of "poor but respectable parentage." The "small boy" arrived from Travancore on a Friday, hence the name by which he henceforth was to be known—*Friday*. A boy with a remarkably intelligent pair of eyes and a slender, but well-knit figure, was Friday. Not a word of English did he speak, neither did he know the use of knife, fork nor spoon, soap nor towel. Totally unsophisticated was Cynthia's *protégé*. And yet his manners were respectful, easy and graceful—the last remaining heritage of race-breeding. The *Ayah*, who with her flirtageous ways, is as a fuse to a train of gunpowder among the men-servants, was given her *congé*, so that the atmosphere of the domestic regions in this respect was cleared and quieted. Friday was to take the *Ayah's* place so far as waiting on his Mistress went.

Friday *did*, and efficiently—well. Naturally

he had to be taught, but he was quick, very quick, and what he once learnt he never forgot. Gradually too, the force of European instruction manifested itself. Friday at mid-day, when he took his second bath, would ask for "Soap, Lady, please, *Pear's* Soap, Friday wanting wash, good wash, English-like." And afterwards when dressed in a clean *nansook kambaya*, drill jacket with pearl buttons, and Turkey-red turban, a smart little page he made. Beneath the turban his pate was shaven, save for a tuft at the back of the crown, which tuft was worn long but coiled up. This mode of *coiffure* marked Friday's *caste*, accentuated by the hieroglyphics in red, yellow and white *chunam* which decorated his brow at the top of the nose. Cynthia had no objection to the latter little embellishment, but she detested the "tuft" and the shaven pate. Friday had glossy, black, wavy hair—why not wear it cut like a civilised being, all round the head? Why not?

She put the question to him. He grinned, salaamed, and shook his turbaned head. Cynthia bided her time and put the question again, more forcibly this time. Again the grin, the *salaam* and shake of the head.

"In the fulness of time," reflected his mistress, "when he is more Europeanised," and Friday was becoming that more and more every day. His progress, too, in English was remarkable, as

Photo. Paté, Ceylon

CYNTHIA'S TAMEL PAGE BOY, FRIDAY

also was his abhorrence of dirt and untidiness. If he saw a speck of dust in a corner out would come a broom, for as he now would say, "Microbe come with dust, Lady, I sweep 'way."

By-and-bye Cynthia deemed the time ripe to allude to the style of *coiffure*. This time, however, two little brown hands went up quickly and held his head as though for dear life, while tears, big crystal tears, filled and over-filled his great black eyes. Not for his life, it seemed, would he part with the "tuft"—his heritage, his caste, his religion. As a compromise, however, he consented to forego the "shave," so that his jetty locks soon became visible beneath the Turkey-red turban, which considerably improved his personal appearance. Cynthia had it not in her heart to desire more.

So exact was Friday in everything he did. In order to replace each little ornament correctly, he would first take a keen survey of the group of ornaments on a table or a what-not before removing to dust, then, with the mental picture before his mind's eye, each would be returned to its right place, and to be perfectly accurate measurements with the duster would be taken. But so quickly, it savoured of slight of hand. The same with regard to table laying and decorations, his intelligent eye speedily perceived the *right* way, adopted, and never forgot it. Taste also was there innate, inherent perhaps, only needing conditions to develop.

"If this be possible, why not the same with the higher moral attributes," reasoned his Mistress. From the first she had endeavoured to inculcate strictness as regards the truth. It had not seemed difficult either. Friday was by nature what is called a "good boy." Only on a few occasions—for instance, when a large jar of jam had been broken into—had he shown symptoms of "backsliding." But Friday was growing older and forming friendships in this, to him, foreign land.

One day his Mistress heard his voice in the compound speaking in *crescendo*, evidently excited, and becoming angrier and angrier. She let it go on awhile, then clapped her hands. Friday obeyed the summons. All in a pant he came, his black eyes ablaze, his red mouth twitching, his whole frame quivering.

"What *is* the matter?" asked Cynthia. She had never seen Friday in such a passion.

The boy cast down his great black orbs sheepishly and began to trifle with a duster in his hand, but made no reply.

"Come, tell me. What are you quarrelling about, and with whom? You know I don't allow strangers and quarrelling in the compound. Speak out."

Friday's coppery skin flushed. He shuffled from one foot to the other. Still he kept silent.

"Now, speak out—I insist," said his Mistress.

Then Friday spoke, anger still in his tone, "That boy, Ma'am" (Cynthia had taught him to say "Ma'am," instead of "Lady," as most native servants do), "That boy, Ma'am, son of sister of butler of Lord Bishop—That son of sister of butler of Lord Bishop——"

"Stop!" cried Cynthia, going over the labyrinth of relationship for the purpose of unravelling, "Son of sister of butler of Lord Bishop—oh! the Lord Bishop's butler's nephew. Well—go on."

"That boy, Ma'am, son of sister——"

"Yes, yes, the Lord Bishop's butler's *Nephew*," interposed Cynthia. It's hard to be patient with the thermometer at 100° in the shade!

"Ne-phew, Ma'am," repeated the boy.

"Well?"

"That—ne-phew boy, Ma'am, saying his Lady more brains got than—than *my* Lady, *I* saying *not*. That ne-phew boy saying his Lady read many English books, newspapers, *I* saying *my* Lady many books, newspapers *write*, more brains got *my* Lady. *Therefore* boys quarrel, Ma'am, angry get."

But the situation was too much for Cynthia. She threw herself back in the lounger and roared with laughter. Just for a minute, Mrs. First Crown Colony Grundy! Then, gathering herself together, that twinkle still there in her eye though, as it rested on Friday's little figure aquiver with the excitement of his late indignation, "Well, it is right you should stand up for your mistress, Friday," she said, "but don't get angry, don't quarrel. Now, go back and tell—the *nephew* of the Lord Bishop's butler that there are different ways of being clever, and that the *best* is to do well what it is our business and our duty to do, so that you and he can be just as clever, too, and one of the cleverest things for all of us to do is to keep our temper. You understand?"

"Yes, Ma'am, I under'tand," picking away at the duster, "*Salaam.*"

After this there was a murmur of voices issuing from the back compound, but all anger was gone out of them.

Friday's vocabulary extended rapidly; day by day he added to it. His mistress, for the fun of it, would experiment with long words. To see the boy prick his ears to catch the pronunciation, then, when he turned his back, repeat the new, ofttimes difficult words in order to stereotype them on his memory, was interesting, to say the least of it. Next day the new word—no matter *how* difficult, was bound to be reproduced.

"Did Punch eat his dinner this evening, Friday?"

"Ab-so-lute-ly, Ma'am," was the reply.

Friday was such an apt pupil, that his Mistress

determined to add caligraphy to his curriculum. "Would *you* like to learn to write?" she asked him one day. Friday's eyes glowed like two tropical suns. That answer sufficed. "Very well, we'll begin to-day—with the orthodox pot-hooks and hangers. I'll set you a copy now, and you can bring it to me when I am at tiffin."

Later on Friday brought his first copy done.

"What on earth are these?" asked his mistress, on beholding the sheet covered over with grotesque caricatures of the originals.

"Or-tho-dox pot-hook and hanger, Ma'am," was the prompt reply.

"Then, for Heaven's sake let us have heterodox," ejaculated his mistress, fanning herself. Next day, upon producing his copy with a *salaam*, he, perking his head on one side, said:

"Ma'am, Friday making het-er-odox pot-hook and hanger, better—not?"

And certainly these were an improvement.

Friday, however, did not make that progress with his pen his Mistress had expected, judging from his other display of quickness.

"Caligraphy is not your *forte*, Friday," she said, wearily, one day when he brought a sheet of paper with *d o g* sprawled all over it. "Not your *forte*," Cynthia heard him repeat after he had said, "No, Ma'am, not my *forte*." At dinner that evening, when Cynthia's husband refused a second supply of the pudding made by his wife—her first (and last) attempt in the culinary art—Friday vouchsafed the remark:

"I under'tand, Sar—not my Lady's *forte*."

And Friday was right.

The problem of creed was vexatious to Friday's budding mind. He often came to his Mistress with perplexing questions concerning the Christian faith, or rather doctrine and dogma.

"Christian man say only one God got, only one religion everybody got, but Christian Baptist man say his God right, his religion right, no other; Wesleyan man say his God, his religion right, no other; Salvation Army man say his God, his religion right, no other; Church of England man say his God, his religion right, no other; and Lady say Christian only one God, one religion got, no other; Friday not under'tand," shaking his turbaned head and looking very puzzled. To cut what might have developed into a lengthy theological disquisition—possibly discussion—Cynthia made answer:

"Be honest, never tell a lie, then you will be a good Christian and—go straight to Heaven."

"Good Christian go straight to 'eaven," repeated the boy, with gleaming eyes. Friday was very keen on becoming a Christian, or on being considered such. He gloried in the *Vale*, the *Pongal* and all Tamil festivities all the same, upon which occasions he liked to wear nice clothes—new if he could get them— and the hieroglyphics on his brow were carefully attended to, likewise his fore-shaven head (spite of his Mistress's disapproval) and the tuft at the back in a well-oiled knot.

"Never tell lie, Tamil boy honest, go straight to 'eaven?" he asked, in order to make sure.

"Certainly. But—how often have I to tell you to aspirate your h's? How the mosquitoes bite!"

Next morning at breakfast: "Will the master take *h*am, *h*omelette, or *h*eggs?" asked Friday, with his big eyes full on his Mistress.

It was while the monsoon was raging that Friday came to his mistress one afternoon—he had been twelve months in their service and was quite a big boy now—came hurriedly in a flutter of excitement. His brother, he said, had arrived unexpectedly from India and had come to see him. Where was he? "There, on back verandah, Ma'am." His large eyes looked twice their size, and under excitement of the unexpected joy there was a restless wildness in them.

"Then" said his Mistress, "Give him a good dinner, and—Friday!" for the boy, after a hasty *salaam* and "T'ank you, Ma'am," was beating a retreat, "Friday, first, let him take a bath—a good *wash*, you know—with *soap*."

"I know, Ma'am—Pear's soap, good vash, I go."

"Stay! Friday. And if his clothes are not respectable give him some of yours. He will want to stay with you until he finds a place, no doubt." Meanwhile the boy was standing first on one foot then the other, a habit of his when excited, his restless eyes wandering anywhere, everywhere except on his Mistress. "Now, go!"

"How happy the child is at seeing his brother!" mused Cynthia, drawing a comparison in her own mind betwixt the "heathen" in this respect and "Christians" of her own kith and kin.

Presently she heard splashing under the stable pump. Her instructions were being carried out. The new-comer was having "a vash." An hour or two later, when the monsoon was for a time abating Cynthia saw the two boys in clean white suits, of her own making Mrs. Colonial Grundy, pass down the compound and out by the gateway.

"Not much resemblance: Mother a Sinhalese probably: he's certainly more Sinhalese than Tamil—the brother," mused Cynthia, anxiously wondering how her husband should be brought home if the monsoon burst again: horses cannot contend with it, neither can the *rickshaw-wallahs*.

However, there was a convenient cessation for awhile. The phaeton was despatched, and her husband in it safely returned. Cynthia told the story of Friday's brother's arrival.

At dinner the boy did not make his appearance.

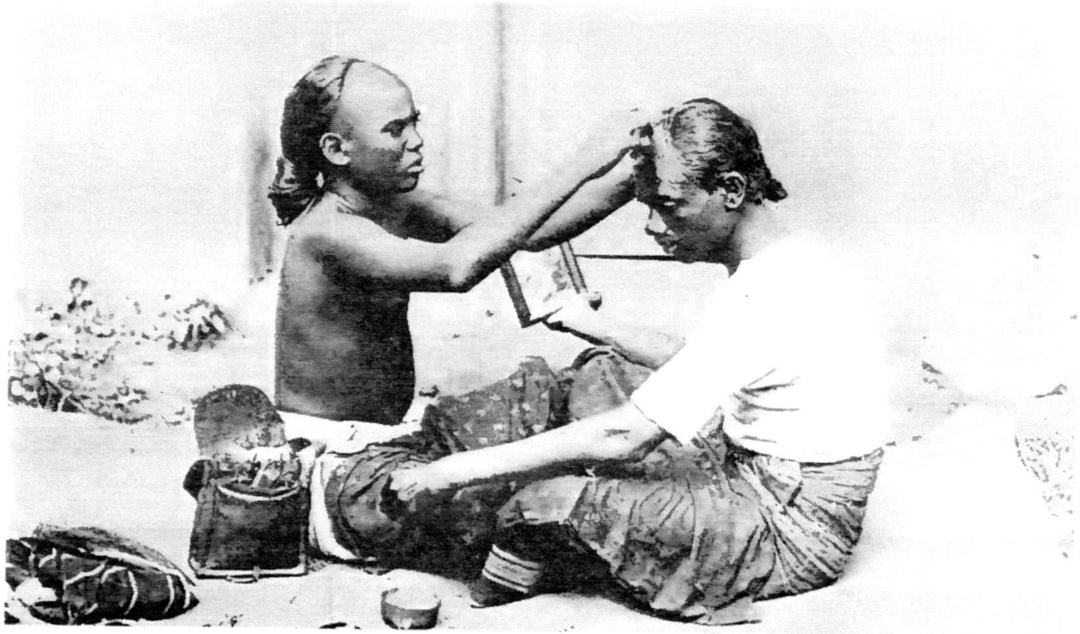

'FRIDAY' HAVING HIS HAIR DRESSED FOR THE '*PONGAL*' ON THE HIGH ROAD TO MOUNT LAVINA

"Has Friday not returned?" Cynthia inquired of the *Appoo*. "Not returned," was the reply.

Last thing at night Cynthia asked again. "Not returned." Cynthia felt anxious.

"Oh, he'll turn up—trust him. They've been overtaken by the rain (the monsoon had burst again) and have taken shelter somewhere. They're all right," was the reassuring response to her anxiety.

Next day, first thing Cynthia put the question again: "Had the boy—had *Friday* come back?"

"Not come back, Lady, Friday nor other boy," answered the *Appoo*—with a smile.

All that day passed and Cynthia's anxiety developed symptoms of alarm.

"I'll send for his friend—the Bishop's butler's nephew," suddenly she said, rising and summoning the *Appoo*, who passed on his Mistress's message to a coolie, being himself of two high a caste to hold converse with inferiors of another bungalow.

The son of the sister of the butler of the Lord Bishop came in due time, grinning. "That boy, Friday, no brother got from India. Other boy, Sinhalese boy, coming to Master's bungalow, eat, bath, take Friday way, gamble, drink—no good Sinhalese boy that. I see Friday going with bad other boy in Friday clothes, I saying Friday 'Come back, not go with bad Sinhalese boy.'

Friday go, Lady—very bad that. Other boy making Friday bad."

Alas! alas! the tale was only too true. Friday had yielded to temptation. Friday had told a lie. Friday had deceived.

The "son of the sister of the butler of the Lord Bishop" was despatched with a *santosum*, and Cynthia felt sad—very very, sad.

Weeks passed by. No other "*podian*" would Cynthia take, although several applied. None other would she have. Cynthia waited on herself.

One evening—a full month later, Cynthia sat writing on the verandah when the nephew of the Bishop's butler reappeared from the shadows of the *suriyas* in the compound.

"*Salaam*, *Lady*," said he.

"What is it?" inquired Cynthia. "Come here."

The boy approached. In a low voice, little more than a whisper, saying: "Lady, Friday come back. I bring?"

"Where is he?" asked Cynthia, starting and straining her eyes to pierce the shadows. "Friday!" She felt, she knew the boy was near.

A lanky ragged form came forward at her call. —came forward, then fell fainting at his Mistress's feet. *It*—was Friday—come back! Only a few weeks, but—a wreck, the skeleton or the wraith of himself. His mistress took him in.

CHAPTER XXIX

Magnificent matrimony — Cynthia attends the nuptials of a Chettie caste bride and bridegroom — *Embarras de richesse.*—How Chettie brides are gowned and gemmed, and conduct themselves—How Chettie bridegrooms conduct themselves—The inevitable W. and S. Primitive but splendid—Cynthia the cynosure of a hundred black orbs—A "golden father" and a "poor little martyr."

NOW it so happened that the daughter of a wealthy Tamil of the Chettie, or money-lending caste, who held an appointment in some way connected with the Government, was going to be married—with enormous *éclat*, as became the contents of the coffers parental, likewise the *caste.*

"Can we not get an invitation?" asked Cynthia, whose imagination immediately conjured up a sketch in water colours of that picturesque object yclept a Chettie, the crown of whose glory consists in the headdress—a sort of inverted coal-scuttle in black satin always, lined with cerise, beneath which droop rings of gold studded with gems—many rings, graduating in size like wheels within wheels, pendant from the ear to the shoulder—water-colour sketches all of them.

Cynthia had made inquiries concerning these Chetties—they fascinated her. Their caste dates from time immemorial as the usurers of India and Ceylon, whose wealth may be likened unto the mines of Golconda. Evidently the caste is in nowise ashamed of such ancient genealogy, else they would not adhere to the ancestral costume as they do—and proudly. Very exclusive indeed is the Chettie *socially*. With the turn of the key on his counting-house is the turn of the key on himself, in so far as all relationship with his private life is concerned. Therefore it was that Cynthia was elated when the invitation to the wedding arrived by post, a satin-faced card printed in silver, which might have borne some resemblance to a less festive occasion were it not for the silver tassel attached, and a trailing spray of orange blossom. It was moonlight when they left home to drive to the "wedding house," as the Sinhalese say—a long drive from the Cinnamon Gardens to Chettie Street, where the caste do dwell. As a matter of fact the rites and festivities had been going on three days and nights. This was to be the culmination and grand finale—at midnight. Some distance ere Chettie Street was arrived at that festivities were going on was substantially apparent. The thoroughfare even at this time of night was thronged; tiny mites of Malay policemen, *bâton* in hand, were about in numbers, to keep order were such necessary. But there being no "Jack Tars" in the throng, that post seemed and was a sinecure. Sinhalese, Tamils, Malays, Hindoos, Cochins, Chinese, all maintained the steady stare of the Oriental, and so far corresponding behaviour.

"Lady going wedding house, Sar? I knowing way wedding house, I showing Master, please." Such offers came from all sides from this curious crowd, which, however, soon became so packed the way, so far as driving was concerned, was impassable. The mare, moreover—fresh from Australia—exhibited symptoms of terror at the unfamiliar objects and scene generally, and began to manifest that terror in such a frantic desperate manner it was advisable to alight, which they did.

"One Brobdingnagian stage. We're behind the footlights, in the thick of the Christmas Pantomime," remarked Cynthia, proceeding to pick up her train, preparatory to proceeding on foot. "What's that?"

"Only Bengal lights. Look at the rockets," was the reply. The crowd now divided their dreamy gaze betwixt the fireworks and the European *Nona* on foot amongst them—such a novelty was this. European "ladies," who never sat in a carriage in their lives in their own country, pretend in Ceylon they have no such things as feet—never had! The *Muttu* leading the fractious *Mascotte* and finding or forcing a way per force of savage yells, Cynthia and her husband followed. The heat was oppressive, not a breath stirred. At intervals a *pandal*, a triumphal arch composed of the illimitable supplies of the cocoanut-palm, adorned the route. Chettie Street, which describes a gentle ascent from bottom to top, was gay with flags, floral and fruit decoration and bunting. At the entrance was a *pandal* of huge dimensions and really artistic structure. A coronet of pineapples decorated the apex of this arch, while the pretty pomegranate blossom and fruit, waxen jasmine and fairy orchids twined about and around, and the wonderful flower of the cocoanut, which resembles a glorified wheatsheaf in the sunlight, gracefully drooped over oranges golden and green. Another *pandal* had a crown of mangoes, another of oranges, another of custard apples, and so on; but all were beautiful in design and most cleverly carried out, the shower bouquets of delicate blossoms and feathery bamboos shimmering in the moonbeams. So on through the throng and the odours up to the verandah of the "wedding house."

Red carpet covered the stone steps, red carpet and *dhurras* covered the verandah, sprinkled all over with rose-leaves, orange blossom and myrtle. The atmosphere was burdened with perfumes.

The host himself—a Chettie in chettie costume—came forward to greet his European guests. A low bow, then a *salaam*, then in response to Cynthia's proffered hand:

"I am happy to welcome you both to the wedding house," said he. "Will the Lady do us the honour to enter?"

"Certainly," said Cynthia, her eye resting on a ruby in one of her host's earrings. The glow of that ruby made a red reflection half way down his white sleeve. Cynthia was not prepared, however, for being detached from her lawful lord and relegated to the regions *and close inspection* of the ladies—dozens of them in Hindoo full dress, blazing with jewels and sucking cardamoms or drinking coffee, or both at once. Ropes and ropes of pearls, rubies, sapphires; not a space on the persons of these Oriental ladies vacant of gems. How meagre Cynthia felt! She had *none*—to speak of. How they must despise her! And yet when dressed for the occasion, in the conviction of her Christian superiority Cynthia had surveyed herself in the cheval glass *smilingly*. She might have felt small now, and yet—what was it that compelled precedence, distinction? The host lingered by Cynthia's chair—the only man in the room—conversing. Subjects of the day—art, music, literature—were touched upon, the Chettie was conversant with all; withal his primitive garb, his mind was cultured up to date. The black orbs of all the ladies rested on Cynthia, their tongues were mute, they resembled lay figures gorgeously arrayed in purple and splendour.

When the host proposed adjournment to the "bridal chamber," Cynthia arose. She wondered what had become of her husband, but passing a doorway caught a glimpse of him surrounded by men in singular combinations of Eastern and Western sartorial array—drinking whiskies and sodas!

Now she found herself in a very large apartment brilliantly draped and decorated, with a daïs at the far end on which sat the bride. Approached by red-carpeted steps, with a canopy overhead, there she sat, the heroine of the night, the heroine indeed of the whole week. A child in years—how tired she looked! A bundle of rich clothes, burdened with jewels! At the foot of the steps a company of native musicians were already in the midst of an overture, which Cynthia was informed was a musical drama descriptive of the young bride's life, past, present, and future—specially composed for the occasion. Cynthia followed the music with rapt attention. Her host had left her now, and she remained alone but for that battery of black eyes. Distinctly descriptive, there were passages in the music of surpassing sweetness, particularly in that part illustrative of infancy and child-life. Later on the turbulence that arose to disturb the tranquillity of childhood had in it much of the spirit of Wagner.

At the termination of each period or "cycle" the orchestra ceased playing. In these intervals the child-bride, escorted by a couple of maidens, was taken to a retiring room, where another robe was added to the one, or two, or three she already wore. In this wise the bulk of the youthful bride perceptibly increased. Furthermore Cynthia remarked an ascending scale to the richness and value of these robes; from sweet simplicity almost unadorned they evolved a worth and a gorgeousness worthy of a fairy-tale princess, or—the daughter and betrothed of an Oriental Chettie.

As the night wore on no less than seven robes enveloped that poor little bride, who really looked as though she would faint or suffocate beneath such *embarras de richesse.* The last robe was of purple plush, embroidered with gold and silver, and studded with gems. Although this poor little martyr, as Cynthia to herself called her, although this most enviable of Chettie kind as her own caste ladies would designate her, spake not a word, her facial expression was expected to respond to the sentiments of the music, a sort of mute acting that had been well rehearsed ere proficiency was attained.

The little bride went through this mute life's drama with punctilious care and precision, as though her salvation depended thereon. At a certain stage—midnight—the music grew slow and solemn and severe, with a little under ripple, plaintive and low. The Chettie host having returned said, *sotto voce*, to Cynthia, "Obedience to her golden-father and lord."

"Who's that?" inquired Cynthia, foolishly forgetful for the moment.

No answer was required, for at that moment the bridgroom entered—for the first time. With his approach, clouds of sandal and incense rose from heated braziers, not so densely however that one could not well perceive the well-set-up young man, well groomed, well whisky and sodaed.

As the clouds of narcotics and spices, frankincense and myrrh, rose on high, Cynthia was told they were symbolic of the ascendency of the male, while the rose petals and sweet blossoms sprinkled in profusion about and around the bride were typical of woman's purity and meekness and lowly worth. Cynthia, accustomed to Society, was glad to know this. There was certainly an offish air environing the young Chettie, who would have been a handsome fellow had he not aped the European.

The bride at the advent of her "golden-father and lord" had risen. Her hands, tiny brown hands laden with rings, clasped on her bosom, she stood—a picture of submission.

The bridegroom then receiving the *Tali* from his patriarchal father commenced to encircle and secure it around his bride's throat, which previously had been divested by one of the bridesmaids of chains of gems, and ropes of pearls. The bridegroom only may perform this ceremony, the placing and securing of the *Tali*. He effected both ultimately after much manlike fumbling and confusion. The key of gold he retained after securely locking the *Tali*. This key must be kept in his possession as long as his life shall last; even so the *Tali* around the throat of his bride.

And now relatives and friends came crowding around, saluting the bride and bridegroom by way of a sniff—they never kiss; many of them bringing presents. The majority of the presents being rings for the bridegroom, the fingers of the young Chettie were adorned to the tips, the overflow being relegated to his "best man."

"Aren't you tired of it?" Yes, Cynthia was very tired. It was 1 A.M. and the heat was overpowering. "I should like to add my congratulations." For this purpose she rose, and the Oriental ladies and gentlemen graciously made way.

Cynthia shook hands with the bride and smiled

her sweetest, words would have been useless. " Poor little martyr ! " she was thinking, " I'd rather see you enjoying yourself with a battledoor and shuttlecock."

To the " golden-father " she said :

" I hope you may have years of happiness, you and your little bride."

" I thank you, Madame. May I offer you a whisky and soda ? " was the acknowlegment, with —not a *salaam*, but a bow. It's a custom of the country in this Paradise of Adam.

CHAPTER XXX

A trip to the Hills—Lovely Nuraliya—Cynthia's finery and its fate—An adventurous journey in a rickshaw with a quartette of *wallahs*—Stranded yet safe—Uda Pussellawa at last!—Explanation—An outbreak of small-pox—Coolies quarantined.

"OF course you often go up to the Hills—impossible for a European to live in Colombo otherwise," Europeans are wont to say.

But there is another side to the possible, as there is also to the impossible. This: can Europeans leave their homes, with easy minds, to the custody of native servants? As a matter of fact perfect assurance cannot always be guaranteed under such conditions in Old England. But in Ceylon——

Cynthia, however, was so "run down" in health after five years' sojourn in Colombo, with very little change, that a visit to the Hills was imperative. *Ergo* she found herself in the train one morning *en route* to Nuraliya, the favourite Hill and Health resort of Ceylon. The railway carriages in Ceylon are built after the model of the Swiss and Scandinavian, and are superior in many ways to those of England. A large restaurant or luncheon and dining car is attached to each train, while the fauteuil-like seats, covered with brown holland, are the perfection of neatness and coolness. Nevertheless, travelling in Ceylon is exceedingly trying. One leaves Colombo, with its tremendous heat, to which one's blood has in time responded, and after three or four hours' travelling finds oneself in another climate. The rapid change of temperature is very trying indeed. Invariably the European upon arriving at Nuraliya is laid up for a couple of days with "chill on the liver"—as Cynthia was. Again, after a week or two's acclimatisation to the Hills, on one's return to Colombo another sudden wrench occurs to one's constitution. But this is anticipating. Cynthia, upon arrival at Nanouya—the station for Nuraliya—was informed that the train, being very late that night, the coach had left; neither was there a vehicle of any description to convey passengers to Nuraliya. "An Hotel? *here—at Nanouya?*" The station-master looked at Cynthia as though he feared she must be crazy.

What should she do? He didn't know—nor care seemingly. Her luggage? That was all right, and would be safe under lock and key in the luggage office. This was a relief, for in that monster basket-trunk were fine frocks and fancies—some fresh from London. *They* would be safe. But herself? What *was* she to do? She had been ill on the journey, and was feeling sick and faint now. But, when a tremendous crash of circumstances occurs one is too stunned to realise one's situation in its dire entirety. Cynthia looked out on the black darkness of the beautiful wooded landscape lit only here and there by a solitary twinkling star, breathing in the invigorating air of the Hills, so cool—it held a snap of frost, which, though it caused a shiver, was delicious—delightful. The sensuous satisfied thus for the time being, her mind troubled itself not with perplexities. She drank in that crisp refreshing air like new wine—alone, for the station-master and porter had retired for the night.

"Are you stranded here—*alone?*" asked a European in a soft voice, the unmistakable voice of a gentlewoman.

Cynthia started, and, turning, beheld the speaker.

"Yes—I suppose so," she answered vaguely. "You are going to Nuraliya of course? Well, I am expecting my brother—he is late, but 'Oh, here he is,'" and the speaker made a rush at a gentleman alighting hastily from a dog-cart. A brief colloquy ensued betwixt them, then, "Will you come with us? We can easily take a turn and put you down at your hotel. My name is——, and this is my brother, a tea planter, whom I have come up to visit. You'd better jump in."

Such kindness! Indeed Cynthia's star—Jupiter the benign—never *would* desert her! Such luck! such kindness! Cynthia *did* jump into the dogcart, and off they drove.

The gloriously fresh air and excitement together kept Cynthia up—indeed that drive was most enjoyable. When, in the midst of it Cynthia told this kind-hearted lady and her brother who she was, it was their turn to express surprise. "This, the literary young woman!" she fancied she read in the minds of both. "Well, she's not half bad, for all that!" Perhaps this addendum though was part and parcel of Cynthia's imagination. However and whatever they thought of *her* *she* thought and still thinks volumes of good of them. And so, in chatting time passed on until these truly good Samaritans put Cynthia down at her hotel door. Cynthia went direct to bed, where she remained a couple of days. The first thing to do upon recovery was telegraph to Nanouya for the precious luggage to be sent up by coach. This was done. No luggage came. Another telegram was despatched. No luggage came. Then Cynthia was advised to go to the coach office. She did. The clerk there said he knew nothing about it, but would "make inquiries," and if it arrived would "see it was sent on."

Still no luggage came. Five days passed.

Cynthia was impatient to press on to her destination—Uda Pussellawa—her friends there having wired for her. She didn't care to go minus her belongings though. Always in hope, ever in expectation, day after day went by. The luggage never came. Then again she went to the office, this time tipping the coachman bountifully and making so sure of success that she asked to book her seat in the coach that went to Uda Pussellawa next day.

No coach was going to Uda Pussellawa next day. When, then? They could not say. What must she do? How could she get there? They shrugged their shoulders. Again she had to wire to her friends. Day after day she went to the office. No luggage, no coach.

After a week of this a bright idea occurred to the clerk. A waggonette had been ordered by a planter to take him to Kandapolla—about midway to Uda Pussellawa—next day. The gentleman would be sure not to turn up, would the Lady be at the office at 10 o'clock to-morrow morning and avail herself of this chance? If the gentleman *did* turn up, well—it was a lady.

Cynthia hastened back, made arrangements with the manageress of her hotel *re* the luggage sending on to Uda Pussellawa as soon as it arrived, and next morning at 10 o'clock was at the office. The waggonette turned up in the fulness of time, but not the Planter. At about 11 o'clock they started—Cynthia taking her seat alone. She was secure for half-way at any rate, sufficient for the time to thoroughly enjoy the drive amid the mountains, notwithstanding the fact of the ramshackle vehicle, called by courtesy a waggonette, that had a way of lopping which was more alarming than comfortable. About two o'clock in the afternoon the driver pulled up. "Kandapolla," said he. "Where?" asked Cynthia, looking round for something in the way of a hamlet at least. "Here, Lady, Kandapolla." A sort of cabman's shelter was all that she could see to disturb the harmony of a peaceful vale surrounded by mountains. "What am I to do?" she asked again.

"Get out, Lady," was the reply. Cynthia obeyed. "Won't you take me farther—on to Uda Pussellawa?" she asked most meekly. The coachman shook his head and expectorated. Now Cynthia had once before found herself in similar straits—in an out-of-the-way part of the Bavarian Highlands at 1.30 A.M. Something had turned up then; something would turn up now. She was feeling hungry, so down she sat, opened her luncheon basket and began to eat ham sandwiches to a tattoo accompaniment of her heels on the road. After some twenty minutes of this a vision seemed to rise from the bowels of the earth. Cynthia at all events had no consciousness of any one's approach until she found a small contingent of coolies and a *rickshaw* in front of her.

"For me, I presume?" said she rising. "Uda Pussellawa, mind. Can you take me? Can you go as far?" She did not want to be stranded again, at a place perhaps where there wasn't even so much as a cabman's shelter.

A volley of Tamil gibberish issued from four red betel-stained mouths, of which Cynthia understood not one word. Therefore, without waste of words and time, she took her seat in the rickshaw, the shafts of which were immediately seized by one coolie, the back by another, the other two coolies holding on to the offside, for a stone in the road might suffice to turn rickshaw, rider and one or two of the coolies may be over the precipice below.

Off they went—like mad. The road was awful. The pace made Cynthia gasp. "Slower! slower!" she cried as up hill and down dale they went, switchback fashion. "Slower! slower!" again and again, but without result. The jolting was such that one could not maintain sufficient mental equilibrum to realise the peril. One false step—one stumble of any one of the quartet of coolies—and over all would go, rickshaw, rider, coolies, all down a precipice of several hundred feet and almost perpendicular.

Cynthia's head went backwards and forwards

like a marionette's worked by a string. She thought her throat must be dislocated and her head whirled off. It was not an agreeable sensation, although the scenery was sublime. Owing to the jerks, her tongue was bitten again and again—almost through. She dug her heels hard into the floor of the rickshaw as a means of maintaining an equipoise, and kept a fixed gaze ahead, while the landscape flashed by—on the one side Nature in all her radiant, exultant beauty, on the other—that precipice, that awful, deadly precipice. Occasionally one or other of the coolies would set up a savage howl, otherwise silence reigned ; nor was there another human being abroad, nor anything in the way of human habitations. So on for a couple of hours or more, when a speck appeared ahead. The speck grew longer, larger and larger until it gained the appearance of a rickshaw and a couple of coolies. Cynthia might—would surely have rejoiced at this advent, and the prospect possibly of a respite, had she been capable of rejoicing, but she was *not*. She was benumbed by this time—indifferent to everything. Both rickshaws pulled up. Cynthia drew a long, long breath.

"Was she alive?" she asked herself. "Oh, yes."

She looked around and her heart expanded to the loveliness of the landscape. She was feeling wonderfully well to. Liver? She *had* none now. "Lady coming in please this rickshaw. Doctor-Master sending bring Lady I finding on road," spoke up the newcomer, approaching with a *salaam*—a *rickshaw wallah* in livery, which proved him to be in private service. All was explained now. Her friends had sent their own rickshaw, in case Cynthia should have been stranded. Cynthia paid off the others with a *santosum* all round, then changed her seat to that of her friend's rickshaw. And on again she went without adventure, without mishap, until she met her friends coming on foot to meet her.

So like a *châlet* in Switzerland was the picturesque bungalow set up in a defile of the mountains! so fresh the air, so charming the scenery, so altogether novel and natural the situation, it was a new world, even to Cynthia, who was familiar with many parts of little-known Europe. Uda Pussellawa, however, is distinctive, and as a health resort incomparable in Ceylon, being not so cool as Nuraliya, yet fresh and cool enough. A pleasant time Cynthia spent here in company of her friends, although—alas for feminine vanity—her precious frocks and finery *never* turned up. She had to wear her travelling garb, with an occasional variation of a blouse of her hostess—a "custom of the country" she was informed when she had at first demurred.

Upon her return—a fortnight later—she found her trunk still under lock and key in the luggage room at Nanouya. Upon opening moreover, she found her new hat—an exquisite creation from London—covered with green mildew. Cynthia hastily closed and locked the trunk. "Why had it not been sent on?"

There had been an outbreak of small-pox amongst the coolies, those unaffected were quarantined. Had the trunk arrived at Nuraliya there would have been no coolies to carry it on to Uda Pussellawa. Perhaps this explained the matter. At any rate, Cynthia had to accept it as explanation, there being no other forthcoming, except it be "the custom of the country" again and yet again.

Photo. Platé, Ceylon

ON THE BEAUTIFUL KELAIYNI RIVER TO VISIT THE FAMOUS KELAIYNI TEMPLE

CHAPTER XXXI

Cynthia's desire to attend a *Jeewama* gratified—*Mascotte* fractious: rider compelled to dismount—Two thousand four hundred *mantras* recited at this interesting ceremony, Cynthia for hours perched on a cocoanut palm stump *without* the charmed circle—*Mascotte* asleep.

ONE morning at daybreak Cynthia had ridden out far along the coast. The weather was glorious, just perfect for riding. On her return, however, somewhere beyond Mount Lavinia, the mare turned stubborn and "up to tricks." Cynthia dismounting, examined the girths, altered somewhat the site of the saddle—everything was right; nevertheless, *Mascotte* continued her tricks as soon as her mistress remounted.

It was tiresome, very. Cynthia was too hot and far too much fatigued to "have it out with the mare." So resigning herself to the situation, she descended and led the fractious Mascotte on foot through the cocoanut-wood.

They had not proceeded far when voices fell upon Cynthia's ear and presently a group of Sinhalese on her vision. As she approached, moreover, the regards of the whole group seemed bent on her, one or two of them—they were all men—waving or, as Europeans would say, " beckoning " to her. Cynthia had been long enough " out " to know that everything goes by the rule of contrary in the East; beckoning is warding off. As she continued to advance, more emphatic became the signals to keep back, until a Sinhalese man, of apparent high caste and importance, came forward and asked in English, " Lady wanting to go this way? Very sorry Lady cannot go. Lady please go other way."

" Why? " asked Cynthia.

" *Jeewama*, Lady," was the answer.

Cynthia's heart bounded. She had heard of that rite called a *Jeewama*—a very exclusive rite indeed. Now was her chance.

" What is a *Jeewama?* " she inquired in her most engaging of tones.

The Sinhalese smiled, but was silent.

" I see you have fixed up some very pretty *Tatawas* (altars)."

The Sinhalese smiled more broadly.

" Lady think *Tatawa* pretty? Lady liking to see *Jeewama* perhaps—not? "

" Certainly I should—very much. I'll secure the mare to this tree. Now—Take me, please, where I can have a good view, and—had you not better tell me first what a *Jeewama* is and *why* it is being held? "

Accordingly, as together they walked on in the direction of the group, Cynthia was informed that the meaning of the word *Jeewama* was to endow with life; that a *Jeewama* can be of benevolent or of malevolent purpose—in either case the ceremony is regarded as very serious, if indeed not sacred; that the site must have been previously charmed—as this had been three nights ago, and that this particular *Jeewama* was to be held in the interests of his own three years old son. At this age the *araksa nool*—a charmed thread with a metal cylinder attached in which is a *mantra* inscribed with a style on a dried talipot leaf, the *araksa nool* and amulet are subjected to the *Jeewama* rite in order to "endow with life," and thus protect the wearer from ill luck during the remainder of his temporal career.

This *Jeewama* then was of beneficent purpose and intent. Cynthia was glad of that. She did not altogether approve of taking part in downright *diablerie*. This was different; her conscience was appeased.

The child—the hero of the occasion—himself would not be present. He was represented by a sketch *en profile*, drawn with a style on a huge haburn leaf, more than life-size, for these haburn leaves often measure four feet in length. This sketch was attached to the trunk of a cocoanut palm immediately behind the principal altar—the *mal bulat tatawa.* So placed was it that it caught the fumes of incense, gungah, resin, cinnamon, saffron—spices, drugs and herbs—a curious compound—blown by the little breeze stirring.

There were five altars in all, all constructed of bamboos, with tasteful embellishments of flowers and fruits and gorgeous blossoms, winding creepers and feathery tamarisk, while spread out on the broad leaf of the plantain were offerings (*dolla*) of food—curry, rice, vegetables and sweetmeats, gifts for the *dewatawa* (lower gods, who always come first) and *dewa* (the higher gods). Not, however, by way of propitiation in this benign case, but merely courtesy, conciliation. On noticing that the "lion's share" fell to the former, Cynthia asked, as usual, the reason why.

"Bad god stronger, Lady: must get more." Wissamony, King of all the Demons, had been already "conciliated"—by gifts, in return for which *wurram* (permission) had been granted. A *Mantra Karayeo* (Priest and Charmer) was as ever to the fore within the charmed circle, which, Cynthia was informed, measured as many feet from the centre either way as there were moons in the child's life. Within, the ground had been duly consecrated with fresh well-water drawn in newly baked chatties and coloured with saffron and cinnamon alternately. This consecration having taken place the spot is prepared and termed *man-*

dala : no heretic foot must enter. Cynthia took up her position on a cocoanut stump at a respectful distance. The ceremony itself was monotonous and far from interesting or exciting. Nevertheless "it was written on her brow," as the Oriental would say, that Cynthia should remain there two mortal hours. No demon nor god was present in person, only their *distria*, which Cynthia translated into thought-projection. The whole rite turned on one pivot. This: should the *Mantra Karayeo* (Priest) of the two thousand four hundred *mantras* he had to recite confuse, forget or mispronounce one word or even one syllable the whole ceremony is useless, worse than useless, for the bad demons then rush in and the purpose is defeated. No sooner did the dial mark the meridian than the *Mantra Karayeo* took his stand in front of the principal altar, a priest of Capuism (worship of the gods) on his right, an astrologer who had cast the child's horoscope on his left, a Buddhist priest behind.

Presently the entire *mandala* (circle) was visible only through the mist of narcotic fumes. The outline of those strangely garbed dark Oriental faces seen through the clouds arising was weird in the extreme. The intoning of the *mantras* that had been going on for more than an hour with a monotonous mesmeric effect had ceased. Silence now reigned, absolute silence, while the narcotic clouds ascended to the sunlit cobalt sky. Silence—for five minutes. Then—a crash, the sound of music—tom-toms, pipes, cymbals, reeds—a gun, whose reverberation caused the mighty ocean to resound, and—all was over. The purpose was achieved. Cynthia, awaking as though from a dream—a weird dream at that—rose, bowed to the company an acknowledgment of their courtesy and returned to find Mascotte, the mare, asleep. Once awake Mascotte's mood for tricks was over—perhaps it was assumed after all, for her mistress's instruction! At any rate the mare permitted Cynthia to mount and ride away now, fast as she could go, to the breakast awaiting both at the bungalow at *Dehiwalla.* Cynthia had realised her desire. She had witnessed a *Jeewama.*

CHAPTER XXXII

The Ceylonese credit-system—Cynthia's resolve—The tea-planter and his story.

THE life of the tea-planter is not all nectar and ninepins, as he would say, in this Paradise of Adam. Some of the bungalows, however, are not only picturesque but comfortable, some indeed are luxurious. But, as a rule, long distances lie between, so that access is difficult if not impossible at times, during the monsoon for instance. Consequently life on many of the estates must be monotonous and may be lonesome. Then comes the fact of having to be out under a blazing sun for hours superintending the coolies at labour—men, women and children of the lowest caste, who live "on the lines" as the row of dingy "shanties" is termed. Very dark, very plain of feature are these toilers on the tea estates, a perpetual frown engenderd by the glare under the blaze of the tropical sun imparting a somewhat forbidding look to their heavy countenances. Some of the Tamil women, however, are very handsome. Stately of figure, beautiful of feature, they walk with the grace and dignity of a queen.

These ladies have a way of calling themselves Mrs. So and So—the name may be of some well-known English or Scotch family—*honi soit qui mal y pense.*

Then there is the miasma, which rises about a foot from the soil, and is visible like a stagnant mist, which, when *not* inhaled, contrives to get into one's system somehow, and malaria is the result. A Government surveyor up in a malarial district once said to Cynthia, "We rarely taste water, having far to send for it, and when we do, the skins may burst or other accident happen before the coolie gets back. What do we drink? Whisky, whisky for ever!" And herein lies another peril, another evil habit too common and too sad, alas! to dwell upon.

And for this parents in England are ready to pay premiums, which they can often ill afford, for their sons to learn tea-planting, deeming it a gentleman's avocation. So it is, when the tea planter does no more than pocket the proceeds. Cynthia had many requests from friends at home for information as to how to get on a good estate as "creeper," but after making herself acquainted with facts her answer was always "Don't."

This lovely Island teems with broken-down gentlemen—planters mostly, some of the flourishing days of coffee, others "might have beens," who sink lower and lower and in many instances

TAMIL WOMEN PLUCKING TEA

but for the kindness of friends might sink lower still. Others again form ties or associations that hopelessly demoralise and drag them down. These lose in time all touch with "home," ay, and all interest in "home." The life of the tea-planter is all very idyllic—*in* the ideal, but those who are not so circumstanced as to become monopolists nor so well off that they can come home every three years or so, to them Ceylon may not prove the Paradise of Adam. After a while the real may prove anything but the ideal.

The system of credit so prevalent, so universal is likewise reprehensible. As a rule the domiciled Ceylonese lives and moves and has his being—on credit!

Once when Cynthia asked a manager at one of the great European stores in Colombo *why* the prices were so fabulously high, his answer was, "Well, you see, Madam, it is such people as yourself and Mr.——who make up for others' bad debts. We *must* charge fabulous prices, because it's only the few who pay at all. Even the life insurance policies frequently made over to us are mostly worthless, for the gentlemen make off to the Straits or Australia and are heard of no more. *You* practically pay their debts." Cynthia from that day made no more purchases in Colombo than were absolutely necessary. All the same, the tea-planter of Ceylon is a very jolly fellow, and withal a gentleman at heart. Here is a story one such told Cynthia bearing on an experience of his own.

The Vedana's Vengeance*

I

"Why don't you chuck it and come up gem-digging with me, old man? Better than that humdrum grind of a Service in this Hades. Try it!"

It was one of those rolling-stones one meets with all the world over who spoke—a handsome fellow of some eight-and-twenty, of good birth, education, brain, and heart, but lacking in stability, which the fact of receiving a remittance from home served but to accentuate.

His friend and former college chum, now third or forth assistant to the Colonial Secretary in Ceylon, knew that, and therefore overlooked a little way he had of being "short." He always paid back, however, when flush with the remittance.

"Chuck it and come up country with me. There's fishing and shooting and big game in the jungle, not to mention rubies the size of a five-shilling-piece, and sapphires and cat's-eyes galore in the beds of these rivers. Phew! We'll top the South African Park Laners yet. Come on."

* By permission of the Editor of *The Crown*.

The Paradise of Adam

Reginald Travers was tempted—sorely tempted. It *was* a humdrum grind in the sweltering heat of Colombo. The clerks, country-born as a rule, were careless and unreliable. The out-station appointments, if cooler, were worse because of their deadly dulness.

"I've half a mind, Jack, but—what would my people say?"

A far-away vision of a vicarage rose before his mind's-eye—father, mother, and a little regiment of olive branches of which he towered the eldest.

"Pah! relations always want to put a spoke in a fellow's wheel. Now, there's my mater—bless her! She thinks I'm wasting my time, actually *wasting my time!* Can't talk her out of it—write, I mean; it's a fixed idea. Fact is she loves her boy; I know that. She would have him always at her apron-strings. But my future, you know—my future!"

Travers laughed, for Jack looked quite grave. But a habitual twinkle soon replaced the gravity. "I 'old by the three 'h's,' as a millionaire once said to me—'henergy, henterprise, and hease at the hend of it.' Millionaires are never your groove men. I quoted this in my last, acknowledging the remit. But—would you believe it?—the dear old lady is still unconvinced!"

The conversation took place on the verandah of the Grand Oriental Hotel, otherwise the G.O.H.

The two had had tiffin together—at Travers' expense, for Jack was "rather short at present." His handsome face beamed with good humour, which goes far towards making up for other deficiencies in this sad world.

Travers laughed, and next moment exclaimed : "Hullo ! Here's old Jimkin's wife, by all that's wonderful ! "

A lady in the latest Parisian fashions came out on to the verandah. "Deuced pretty girl with her, by George ! " Jack whispered.

A slight twitch puckered Travers' brow, and off went his pith hat, which salutation both ladies exchanged. "One of the leaders of society here," he added *sotto voce*.

"Whew!" responded Hartley. "And the girl? *She's* good form."

"Oh ! *she's* a lady—the General's daughter, Miss Tremayne. Society's mixed here."

There was a pause as the ladies passed by.

"But, tell me more of your plans," resumed Travers. "The gem-digging game—it sounds exciting, and this verandah's dull when there's no steamer in."

The friends settled down to talk over Jack's "latest," with little or no interruption. It was nearly four o'clock when Travers recollected there was an ordinance demanding his attention at the Secretariat and that he must be off before the clerks left. Jack was leaving by the evening train from the Fort.

"Good-bye, old chap; mind it's a bargain. Your six weeks' leave you'll spend with me, or part of it. I'll hurry on the habitation. Till then —ta-ta. Take care of yourself. Don't get entangled in any double harness business; you always were inclined that way. Psha! a wife hampers a man so. 'If she be not fair for me.'— By Jove! that Miss—Miss—What's-her-name with old Jimkin's wife, don't you know, *she's* ripping! Buried among these niggers makes one sentimental, and sigh for the touch of a vanished hand and the sight of a white face still. Not quite correct, but near enough. Don't forget to write, and all my good advice. Can't mount all those steps. By-bye!" Thus on the steps of the Colonial Office they parted.

II

Two months had elapsed, and Reginald Travers found himself again with his friend up-country. Not a white face was within many a mile of the mud-and-wattle bungalow Jack had had erected in the jungle near one of Ceylon's beautiful rivers.

Jack was gem-hunting. Not had much success as yet, but was "in hopes." Meanwhile he lived on his means—the remittance from home and the products of his gun and line.

But Bass is a rupee a bottle and whisky eight, so that when Travers came up he found his friend "rather short."

A week later the remittance arrived, and Jack's crest went up.

"Delighted to see you, old man," had been the greeting. "Same to you, Jack," and both were genuine as men only can be.

What with shooting, fishing, and hunting the days passed pleasantly enough. Jack was proficient on the banjo, too, and sang coon songs in the moonlight to the chattering of monkeys, shrieking of parrots and peacocks, snarling of jackals, ferocious maul-wowing of wild cats, and occasional trumpeting of elephants. Stretched outside on their loungers, with their revolvers at hand, there was fascination in the very fact of the proximity of peril. Oh, the charm of a tropical night in the jungle! Travers gave himself up to it for the first week.

"I say, Jack, what about the gems?" he asked one day.

"Oh, they're all right, awaiting our leisure. There's a curious old temple I thought we'd go to see to-morrow. Our *tats* will carry us in the cool of the morn. Some fifteen miles, but it's worth seeing. You have a passion for antiquities—or used to have. But, like most Europeans out here, I don't suppose you've even heard of this."

Travers confessed he had not. "Thought so, therefore I held the expedition in reserve for you, old man. Europeans come and go and know no more of these places than if they'd never been. Right you are; we'll fix it for the morn." And they did.

Riding at dawn is delightful in Ceylon, the air is so fresh, being uncontaminated as yet by the breath of humanity.

When within a mile of their destination Jack suddenly exclaimed: "Hullo! there's the chap I chucked off my verandah the other day!—the *Vedana* (or headman). He came skulking round and cringing until I couldn't stand it any longer. Off he went, towel and umbrella! Didn't know he hung out here."

A Sinhalese, fresh from his morning bath, with long, flowing hair, surmounted by the comb which distinguishes the *Vellala* caste, greeted them with an obsequious *salaam*. At the same time a lurid light latent in every native's eye gleamed for an instant when it lit on Hartley.

"Is the *Mahatmaya* going to the temple?" he asked, addressing Travers.

"We are," was the reply.

"Then, if the *Mahatmaya* will permit, the *Vedana* will show the way."

"Bah!" scowled Hartley. But Travers, being

in the Government service, knew the meaning of that word policy.

"Very good—lead on, Macduff," said he.

At the foot of some three hundred and seventy steps cut in the rock they drew rein. On the summit stood the ancient temple, erstwhile Hindū, now Buddhist, or, to be exact, a combination of the two. The steps were irregular and shallow, and now that the sun was well up it was hard climbing. They heaved a sigh of relief when they reached the top.

A couple of black eyes belonging to a yellow-robed monk had been watching the ascent behind a *grille* in the *Pānsala*. The *Vedana* undertook to make the request to see over the temple, and soon returned with the monk in charge, followed by an attendant acolyte with the keys.

In spite of dust and dirt—the accumulation of centuries—the frescoes beneath retain their wonderful colouring. Scenes from the *Ramanayana* and other sacred epics are, with the later Buddhist hells, graphically depicted, while all sorts of weird and grotesque faces and figures look out from cobwebs and irrepressible vegetation in the friezes and gargoyles.

The first chamber contains the throned daïs where the High Priest Sumungala officiates once a year, and in niches are hung images of the Buddha in proximity to Hindū gods, while many

Photo. Platé, Ceylon

A FOOT-MOUNT CUT IN ROCK LEADING TO AN ANCIENT TEMPLE, ERSTWHILE HINDŪ, NOW BUDDHIST

altars, quaint and artistic, filled with floral offerings and surmounted by lamps of smouldering incense and powdered resin and sandal, charge the heavy torrid atmosphere with suffocating and narcotic properties. The shrine, however, is three chambers removed, and approached by a formidable door with triple locks. The walls are lined alternately with ivory, silver, and gold *en repoussé*, each panel being a foot in width.

As the party entered the little light coming in through the shuttered *grille* fell on an image on a central altar, directly upon the blood-red gems of a necklace and obliquely upon an immense cat's-eye on the brow, which latter reflected the rays in long streams of effulgence that followed the eye turn which way it would. The monk unbarred the shutter, and gradually the sanctuary, with its gold and silver images, came into distinct view. Hundreds of tarantula spiders, running, jumping, ran helter-skelter, in dread terror at being disturbed.

No sooner was the *grille* uncovered than a crow came "quark-quarking," and, forcing itself between the bars, in its blindness in coming from the glaring sunlight going bang against Jack's eye. He struck out at the bird with his riding-whip. "Brute!" he exclaimed. "Nearly knocked my eye out."

After this they gave their whole attention to

the images—images of massive gold, studded with priceless gems, notably the Buddha with the necklace of rubies and the cat's-eye on the brow.

"By George!" said Jack aside to Travers. "Now's our time, old man! And—*what* a saving of labour! Only a little legerdemain's required and our Park Lane mansion's secured!"

Travers laughed, then more seriously said, "What an amount of good might not that string of rubies alone do to a host of poor, starving wretches during a famine, say, out here—eh?"

"Will the *Mahatmaya* look at this?" spoke the *Vedana*, turning from the monk to whom he acted as interpreter. *This* was a life-size figure of the Goddess Kali, with the scarlet tongue and emerald eyes, side by side in a glass case with *Pattini*, wearing armlets of gold and a *tali* bedizened with jewels, her ruby eyes looking obliquely on all around with a hideous effect. No demons or evil deities in Hindū mythology can compare in wickedness with the "eternal feminine."

"Shouldn't care to encounter these ladies," said Jack. "Let's get out of this or we'll have nightmares for a month. Whew! What's that?" There was a sudden noise.

"Only the crow. He's out, though I didn't see him go."

"Good luck to him. We'll be off too."

Meanwhile a brisk duologue was going on between the monk and the *Vedana.*

"Tell that chap to shut up and show the way out, Travers." But, instead, monk, acolyte, and *Vedana* were gathered round the central altar.

"The ruby necklace, *Mahatmaya,*" said the latter.

"Well, what about it?" asked Travers.

"Gone!" said the *Vedana.*

"*Gone!*" echoed the Englishmen—*gone!*"

"By the powers, yes—*Gone!*"

Each looked at the other.

Here was the image, but the necklace—where? Jack struck a match and searched about. A hurricane lamp was fetched from the *Pansala* by the acolyte. Not there. The ruby necklace was gone.

Who had taken it?

This thought was uppermost in the mind of each. The *Vedana* remembered overhearing what Jack had said in an undertone to his friend—a native never forgets; Travers remembered too. But no! Jack was incapable of *that.* He speedily banished the idea. Nevertheless the fact remained. The ruby necklace was gone, and Jack—*Jack had handled it last!*

III

One morning while taking their *chota hazira* on the verandah a missive was delivered into the hands of Jack Hartley. On opening he found it to be a summons to appear in the Police Court, Colombo, to answer a charge laid against him of the theft of a ruby necklace from the sacred image in the shrine of the temple at Narawella. Jack first opened his eyes, then his mouth, and laughed uproariously as he handed it to Travers.

"Just like the Sinhalese; they're litigation mad! Ever on the look-out to 'take a case,' as they put it."

"But this is too much," Travers replied.

"A joke, my dear fellow—a joke, a break in the monotony of—ahem!—gem-digging," returned Jack, going on eating his *appas*. "Stay, here's something else. Why, it's another for *you*. 'As aider and abetter in the act!' By—the Goddess Kali, scarlet tongue and all! Ha, ha, ha!"

Nevertheless Travers did not appreciate the joke as his friend did. He thought of his post under Government, thought, also, of a pair of sweet eyes associated with the *billet* he had received but yesterday, and which had reposed under his pillow all night—thought, and knit his brows.

"Confounded nuisance!" he muttered, biting away at his moustache.

"Not a bit of it, man; an excellent excuse for a holiday. Gem-digging palls—after a time. When are we to show up—the 26th? We'll make a week of it at the G.O.H., and add another to the list of one's experiences in the East.

. . . . . .

The 26th found them both in the Police Court, Colombo, unrepresented by "proctors," as solicitors are called there; the affair was too absurdly trivial, as Jack maintained.

Travers was not so confident, and was wearing a somewhat anxious face. "Buck up, old man; best joke I've known since I set foot in this Garden of Eden," whispered Jack as the *Vedana* entered the witness-box.

They were both unprepared for this witness repeating what it seemed he had overheard Hartley say to his friend concerning the ruby necklace whilst inspecting it in the temple.

"The mean hound!" muttered Jack, while Travers's countenance from amazement soon relapsed into real gravity.

"These gentlemen were gem-digging?" questioned the magistrate.

The witness smiled. "No, sir."

"But that was their object in being there?"

"They *said* so, sir."

"But Mr. Hartley? *He* had been at it some time?"

"No, sir;" and that smile, if inscrutable, was pregnant with deep meaning.

"Then you mean to aver that nothing in the way of gem-digging had been done or even begun?"

"Nothing"

The monk and the acolyte confirmed the fact of Hartley's handling the necklace last and speaking in a low tone to the other gentleman, while a crowd of witnesses standing in the body of the court were ready to support the "ostensible" gem-digging.

The magistrate looked perplexed, and seemed relieved to dispense with the matter by stating the case was beyond his jurisdiction—a case for the Judicial Court, in fact.

This was not a satisfactory termination by any means. Even Jack's joviality received a shock.

Once he caught the *Vedana's* deep, unfathomable eye, and the pale smile on that placid countenance exasperated him beyond endurance. "I could shoot that rascal!" he muttered. "As for this crowd of witnesses, I never set eyes on one half of them before—scoundrels and liars all of them!"

Travers was staggered—bewildered! An accomplice to a thief! God! Was anything more bizarre? Surely the judge would see the grotesqueness of it! Surely——

But this was not England—this was Ceylon; an enormous gulf lay between! And the jury! Travers was not reckoning on that. And his chief, and his *confrères* in the Service, and Mamie

Tremayne, and the austere General, *her* father; surely—surely they would see the utter ridiculousness of it! Nevertheless it was—awkward.

He had proposed being in *Nuraliya* for the *Gymkhana*, and now might be detained or summoned back to Colombo over the absurd business. "Confoundedly annoying, to say the least of it, Jack."

"Buck up, old chap. And now for mulligatawny, prawn curry, Bombay ducks, papadas, and chutney, a votive offering to the God Digesto. Boy!"—to a native waiter—"whisky and so-da!"

Hartley did not go back. He had had enough of gem-digging for a time, he said, but remained at the G.O.H. in wait for his remittance, getting both board and lodging on credit in the orthodox way out there in Ceylon. Travers went up to *Nuraliya*; Mamie Tremayne was there.

The day appointed found them both at the District Court however, on the grave indictment of having committed theft at the Narawella Temple. Much the same evidence was gone through again—the Englishmen being represented by counsel this time—only that the crowd subpœnaed to prove that no gem-digging had ever been attempted was made up of different personalities, a mere detail in Ceylonese litigation.

All the accused could say in reply was that they knew not what had become of the ruby necklace. It was there around the Buddha's throat, and had been handled by both, Hartley last, who on oath declared he had "put the thing back." Then their attention had been given to other things, and on returning some one—the *Vedana*—had remarked the necklace was gone! Yes, certainly Hartley had spoken thus about it to his friend, but in joke. Travers testified to his comrade's habit of speaking heedlessly in joke. Everybody acquainted with Jack Hartley knew that way of his; it was his nature. Had he never been known to put such careless observations into action? Most decidedly not!

The *Vedana*, recalled, dwelt on the low mysterious tone of the accused's voice when making those remarks, "Now's our time," &c., &c., a mere whisper for his frend's ear alone. Did the witness actually see the suggestion put into practice? The *Vedana* smiled that inscrutable but significant smile of his, whereupon counsel for the defendant got up and protested against this witness's evidence as prejudiced, seeing that he cherished ill-feeling towards the accused on account of——

But the judge objecting, the sentence was left unfinished. That question was put again. Did the *Vedana* actually see the accused's suggestion put into practice? The witness wriggled about, smiled, then that latent lurid light gleaming in his eye, he answered, "Yes, I saw-——"

This was too much for Jack. He roared at the

top of his voice, "That man's a rascal, a scoundrel, a liar!" At a sign from the judge order was speedily restored.

Travers's counsel, in defence, stated, how it came about his client was there, acknowledging at the same time that up till then no effort in the way of gem-digging had been made; as a matter of fact, his client regarded it more as a holiday, as his friend—well, his friend was not given to taking things seriously.

The two counsel were well matched, both able and eloquent, the one Sinhalese, the other Burgher, as the Dutch descendants are called. The jury, made up of mixed blood, if partial, maintained stolid countenances until the court rose. After a brief discussion the case was adjourned for that day week.

During those seven days Travers endured a martyrdom. His was a thin skin, and he imagined slights if they did not actually exist. When they met on Galle Face Drive he thought Mamie Tremayne's bow a little stiff. His chief's eye never met his. Was it purposely done? It seemed the buzz of conversation at the club abated on his entrance.

Even Jack's society jarred upon him. Jack was so cocksure of the game being exploded. But Travers had been the longer of the two in Ceylon. And this *Vedana!* Jack had ordered him off the verandah, calling him a "skulking hound" or something of the sort. Vengeance! Was not that the interpretation of that strange light which comes at times into the native's eyes? He (Travers) could read the whole, clear as noon-day But the law——

The day at length dawned. Travers had worked himself up to a pitch of feverish anxiety, Hartley of wrath.

What would the issue be? Would he (Travers) be requested to "send in his papers"? What if his career be terminated—thus! his life blighted, his hopes crushed, his future——

Justice? In England now——

"Come on, old chap, the buggy's waiting. I'll thrash that rascal within an inch of his life yet, or perish in the attempt. Wait till I get my remittance!" It was Jack *en route* to the District Court. Once there the judge was soon to arrive, looking unusually grave.

On the court resuming, the entire morning was devoted to the defence. Nevertheless, notwithstanding the eloquent speech of counsel, the case looked black against the accused Englishmen. Tiffin time came and went. Counsel continued his address, but had not proceeded far when a note was handed to the judge—a telegram bearing an up-country post-mark. His lordship, opening, perused, just a shadow of a twinkle coming into his blue eyes as he read and read again. Then bending forward he whispered to the clerk, after which, clearing his throat and with an apology to the advocate, he spoke slowly.

"Crow with ruby necklace round throat alighted on verandah. Shot crow; secured necklace.

A buzz went through the court.

"Now, I wish myself to put a question. Did any one see a crow in the shrine that day?"

"Yes, yes," from Travers and Hartley in a breath. "Here's the mark of its beak when it nearly pecked my eye out. You remember, Travers?" Travers *did* remember. So did the monk, likewise the acolyte, and lastly the *Vedana* thought he remembered also.

"Then the charge is cancelled. The case is dismissed. *The crow was the culprit.* The necklace shall be restored."

No ovation did the acquitted then receive, for their compatriots were conspicuous by their absence. Alas! for the *majority* of humanity. But later, when the news had spread like fired gunpowder, Travers and Hartley found themselves besieged with sympathisers.

"My heartfelt congratulations, Travers!" The General was the speaker. Mamie, standing by his side, looked her gladness and her womanly sympathy. As a matter of fact, Travers in *this* suit progressed by leaps and bounds, for there is no surer road to a *true* woman's heart than to excite her compassion.

"That awful *Vedana!*" she exclaimed. "And

what a dear, sensible old crow to bring it back and make it all square! Oh, I—I"—and a suspicion of tears came into her pretty eyes. She turned away.

"I was only going to say I wish Mr. McDougall hadn't shot it. I should have liked to keep it as a pet."

Travers went that evening and gave an order for a crow fashioned in gold, with ruby eyes, and necklet, to be made as speedily as possible. This he sent to her next week, with a request that she should wear it "as a charm—for *his* sake." Then when he saw her next, the first thing he saw was —the crow!

"It's a case, Travers. That's plain as a pike-staff," commented Jack. "I'm not going to eat the gooseberry pie, old man, and gem-digging's played out: I'm off. *Where!* Why, to Africa and the gold-fields. I'll entertain Mr. and Mrs. Reginald Travers—ahem! His Excellency, perhaps, by then—in my Park Lane mansion yet! I wish that remittance would come! I'm rather short at present. Ah, thanks awfully, old man, and many happy returns—I mean, best congratulations. Heigho! It's a hard life, this gem-digging, gold-hunting business. I've half a mind to chuck the whole game and settle down. Boy, whisky and soda—for two!"

CHAPTER XXXIII

The "little tin gods of Ceylon"—The change at Aden with the *cummerbund*—Blue blood and brains, and "stars" that set—Will East and West blend?—What Cynthia's severe experience taught her—Where was the bird of Paradise? and Betsy?—The curious reply: It's a "custom of the country."

CYNTHIA cannot bring these reminiscences to a close without mention of the Civil Servants of Ceylon—those "little tin gods," as Kipling aptly designated them.

The Civil Servants are the "blue blood" of Ceylon—particularly in their own estimation. They take precedence both of the naval and the military.

One becomes conscious of this fact immediately upon leaving Aden on the voyage out, for there are sure to be some of the "blood" on board.

"What's the matter with the men?" asked Cynthia of the captain in whose care she first went "out." The captain smiled. "Look at them!" she added, waving her hand in the direction of two or three couples swaggering along the deck in what, to her unsophisticated mind, was a curious sort of dinner dress.

"What are they walking like that for? And listen! What a drawl! They weren't always like that. What's the meaning of it?"

The captain laughed right out. Cynthia sat at his right hand at table—in spite of the other ladies petitioning for a change of seats on leaving Port Said. The captain was often amused at her *naïf* remarks and pertinent (perhaps Mrs. Colonial Grundy would say *im*pertinent) comments. He was now.

"This, I see, is your first introduction to the Anglo-Ceylonese *in the East.* With the *cummerbund* and white dress jacket he blossoms forth on leaving Aden. There he goes—swagger, drawl and all," was the Captain's reply.

"Good *Hea*-vens!" said Cynthia—no more.

But she *thought*—a chapter!

That there are brains among the Civil Servants of Ceylon is, however, an incontrovertible fact—even among the cadets.

These rise and in some instances distinguish themselves in more ways than one. For example, the gentleman who, to gratify the intellectual taste of a certain Governor of the Island *pro tem.*—who had an earnest desire as well as a human sympathy with, an earnest intellectual as well as a humane desire then—to behold a descendant of the deposed King of Kandy, dressed up in costly raiment and jewels, a low caste but good-looking Tamil tea-plucker to play the part. So well was the part played that His Excellency unsuspecting manifested great interest in the "Princess," descendant of a royal but ill-starred house, and the whole occasion—a very festive one—passed off with *éclat.*

Alas and alas! The ingenious device of the Civil Servant was found out. Herein lay the mischief. His papers were requested to be sent in. And so the Civil Service lost a star. Other stars likewise have risen to set prematurely; for instance, a Servant of the Government who, desiring to take unto himself a second wife while yet his first wife lived, undivorced, sought the novel expedient of exchanging the religion of his forefathers and compatriots for that of Mohammed. By so doing his desire was gratified—legalised—in a way. The idea spread. Like a flash of lightning it brought inspiration to other masculine minds.

The Government, fearing a wholesale flight to Moslemism, requested the originator of this brilliant idea to "send in his papers."

Another "star" in Ceylon's Civil Service had set. And yet the Service survives and flourishes, fresh blood always coming in; red blood, "black" blood and mixed; all, however, considering itself "blue" in this First Crown Colony! Its ramifications extend all over the Island, the best perhaps, and of most practical human value being the medical organisation.

Hospitals there are in all parts of Ceylon ably presided over by qualified medical men, all under the direction of a Principal Civil Medical Official, the present officer being deservedly one of the most honoured men in the Island.

The military are the military all the world over—for chivalry incomparable. But to sum up.

East is East and West is West,
And never the two will blend,

as Kipling says. This is true. Cynthia, humanitarian to her finger-tips, tried it. But no! the Oriental and the Occidental may meet, but never mingle. Their minds view things from different angles. To the European, the Oriental way is the way of topsy-turvydom ; probably ours is to them. Nevertheless the magnetism of the East is subtle and strong, narcotic one might say ; for does it not numb some faculties while it evokes and excites others ? If one needs a bath of Lethe one should go to the East. If one is desirous of developing certain psychical faculties dormant in the workaday West one should—go to the East. Other moods, other capacities, faculties, potentialities are awakened there—providing, of course, one does not relapse into the condition of inertia, physical and mental, as so many, perhaps *most* Europeans, out in Ceylon do—especially women.

Now Cynthia always endeavours to carry out that trite old saying, "When in Rome do as the Romans do." One need not be so literal as to eat with one's hands. But to adapt oneself is prudent—or to *try* to. At all times and above all things not to carry one's hard and fast habits and customs and dogmatise to those who all the while are scarcely in doubt of one's sanity. This, many Europeans do. Missionaries may preach; everything remains as it was—*below the surface*—and some time or other the best "converted" will fall back to his own flesh and blood, for blood is thicker than water, heredity more potent than preaching.

On the other hand—for are there not always two sides to a question?—Oriental philosophy (not religion) is pure, unselfish, sublime—sublimated agnosticism, one might say. Futhermore, every Oriental is a born philosopher. He has a moral axiom to meet every emergency and is never nonplussed. Talleyrand might have learnt much from the Oriental, for his axioms always tend in the right direction, that is selfward, and emanate likewise from his own personal point of view. A study, an intensely interesting study, is the Oriental, a product of the ages, of the soft sunlit scenery, of the physically enervating yet thought-inspiring clime. He meditates asquat on his heels for hours, his eyes gazing far away, into infinity apparently. The European looking on thinks him stupid, bovine. *Is* he? All the while thoughts are animating his subtle mind, a reservoir too deep for the average European to fathom, with all his "cram." But the European of reflective tendency is speedily caught in the mental magnetism of the East. And then comes the fascination. Then, inner eyes seem to open, hidden faculties awaken, psychical senses unfold, and another life—a life within this life—is discovered or revealed. Many Europeans experience this in its *initial* stage in a greater or a lesser degree. If the former, they can never forget it—*never shake it off.* If their temperament be æsthetic, it comes to them as food-light-air does to their material requirements, only that, being more subtile-ethereal, it possesses greater charm, greater fascination than any more substantial sustenance. Herein lies the *true* "fascination of the East."

Even those who live what may be termed the ordinary, if not vulgar life out in Ceylon, in the midst of the pretentiousness there runs a *fugue* throughout the "loud pedal" music of their existence, a *fugue* the most sensuous and least witted are conscious of, although they may not be possessed of the higher sensibility to comprehend. To those others, who, alas! are in the minority in this up-to-date mushroom age, the Orient is a world of dreams, Ceylon a Paradise, a Paradise not of Adam only, a Paradise of Eve it might be, were the law respecting woman altered.

Cynthia, seated as usual on the verandah, her companion Punch, alas! no longer by her side, was thinking all this over in her mind.

She had been "out" now seven years—a period in which, 'tis said, every atom and molecule has changed. Had Cynthia changed? Physically perhaps, but in heart not, although her mind had grown, expanded, so that she could grasp many a complex thing that her understanding had stumbled against erstwhile. The sunlit scene was just as beautiful before and around her as on that day of her advent seven years ago.

But—"Where was the Bird of Paradise?—and Betsy?" she asked herself. Had it all been a dream? Had she not till now awakened from that drowsy slumber that had overcome her on the verandah that first afternoon of her arrival in Ceylon? It seemed so. Looking back, the whole seven years appeared nothing more than a dream—a beautiful dream in part—an idyl—with touches of comedy, ay, and tragedy too. In retrospect she went over it all again.

"Where is the Bird of Paradise—now?" Cynthia asked herself again.

The only response was the "quark-quarrk" of the crows. Save for the crows Cynthia was alone. But no! a voice presently fell on her hearing:

"Lady, carriage come take Lady 'way." Cynthia arose, took one last look around the bungalow, then stepped out and into the *gharry* which was to convey her to the Colombo landing-stage, whence a boat would carry her and her luggage to the *P. and O.* steamer *en route* to Old England.

No sooner had she taken her seat in the *gharry* than a little forest of bare brown arms encompassed her and a chorus of voices exclaimed:

"*Santosum!* Lady, *Santosum!*"

Cynthia threw them coins—"a custom of the country" in the Paradise of Adam.